77 DAYS
in my head

by CITIZEN

F

77 Days in My Head by Citizen F

ISBN 978 1 7396674 7 4

Copyright on all original materials in this magazine remains the sole copyright and property of the author Citizen F, under the Copyright, Design and Patents Act 1988. No part of this work should be reprinted without the permission of the author.

Photography and Artwork by Citizen F (unless otherwise stated).

Poetry by Citizen F (unless otherwise stated).

Cover Design by Citizen F.

First Published in the UK in 2024 by Caldew Press.

Caldew Press
Tolivar
12 St George's Crescent
Carlisle
CA3 9NL

Caldew Press email: caldew-press@outlook.com

www.caldewpress.com

Printed by 4edge Ltd, UK.

The author would like to thank the following:

Phil Hewitson and Caldew Press for their courage and support.

My darling wife and family for their patience and understanding.

Worldometer - their statistics were an invaluable resource.

Those Facebook friends whose comments have been included here.

You can contact Citizen F at citizenfpoet@gmail.com

CALDEW PRESS

77 DAYS
in my head

by CITIZEN

F

Above me whistles the wind,
causing leaves to fall from sibilant trees,
whilst beneath me, from the depths, I hear
the yelping of strangled dogs.

    From 'UNDERTOW'

INTRODUCTION

A novel coronavirus had initially come to the attention of the World Health Organisation (WHO) on 31st December 2019. The first cases of transmission of severe acute respiratory syndrome coronavirus 2 (SARS-CoV-2) within the UK were confirmed in late February 2020. Coronavirus disease 2019 (COVID-19) is the name given to the disease that is caused by the virus.

On 11th March 2020 the WHO declared the Coronavirus outbreak a pandemic. The UK introduced measures to protect the National Health Service - measures commonly referred to as 'lockdown' - on Monday, 23rd March 2020.

This book tells the story of one man and his family during 77 days of lockdown. The journey starts six days into the first lockdown, on Sunday 29th March, after a tumultuous week and little rest for some of the household in the sleepy West Cumbrian harbour town of Maryport. Sometimes poignant, sometimes sardonic, often light-hearted and, inevitably, having the occasional need to be deadly serious, it celebrates the banal and the mundane as well as capturing some of the news of the day and the spirit of the country as the story of the pandemic - a truly shared experience - unfurls before us.

A journey of self-discovery and re-evaluation, it pulls no punches and gives a deeply personal insight into one man's struggle - from juggling with 'knowledge' gleaned from a crash-course in online research and an obsession with World rankings to dealing with conspiracy theories, paranoia, mental health, the burning frustration of powerlessness and a responsibility to the rest of his family to 'keep it all together'.

The book is peppered with poems - either hand-picked from history or written by the author or his wife - photos taken exclusively in Cumbria on or around the actual diary date and other 'arty stuff' deemed suitable to fill the occasional blankness on a page!

I dedicate this to a father I never knew: William (Billy), who died aged 28.

'BILLY'

I was married by the time I was your age, Billy,
But by then you'd fathered a child
And shortly after you left us, Billy -
Me and my mum, your bride.
You left me no memories to savour, Billy,
But I imagine you so meek and so mild.
I don't know why you left us, Billy.
Natural causes? No, suicide.

....

EVEREST

2020 March 13

Unlucky for a privileged few
Nepal's government locked down Everest
There will be no climbing season this year
Just a small team installing the world's highest 5G masts
And marking 60 years since the first North side ascent
By a Chinese mountaineer

The spectacular snow-capped peaks
One hundred miles from 'The City Of Temples'
Were clearly visible from Kathmandu
For the first time in decades
A benefit of the pandemic
To reduced pollution levels due

In May 2019 there had been eleven deaths
Inexperience is said to have caused that spike
A short weather window and novice climbers
Are a lethal mix - this is no Lakeland hike!
Just enjoy the views, don't mind the dead bodies
As to breathe the thin air you struggle
Leave it to others to calculate what's needed
To keep you alive and with oxygen levels juggle

We may all now be in our Everest summit phase
Everyone walking a fine line between life and death on life's edge
People with large amounts of disposable income these days
Are quite literally dying in the queue to get to the top - a knife's edge
Cutting through their curiously inward-looking, self-centred need here
To risk life and limb to share the first 5G selfie on social media:
"Just enjoying the views, not minding the dead bodies
As to breathe the thin air I struggle
Leaving it to others to calculate what's needed
To keep me alive and with oxygen levels juggle"

The true achievement of any Everest climb
Is almost always that of the support team that you can count on
It's the same as it ever was and will be for the rest of time:
Poor people dragging rich people up the mountain

==

PART ONE

DAY 1

Sunday was a funny one.

I came across the poetry anthology *Poetry For A Purpose: Saving The World With Words* (Caldew Press) that I've contributed to, available to buy for a tenner on Amazon. I don't have my free copy yet and I didn't know it was available to buy/pre-order now. I also discovered that I appear to have been banned from a local Facebook group, to which I have been regularly contributing photos recently, after my last pic of a beach/cloudscape apparently breached guidelines. No worries!

I had got up for a drink of tap water in the early hours of this (Monday, Day 2) morning. It tasted like no water I have ever drunk anywhere in the world, ever. It was sweet - but not in a good way. I googled what it might be - calcium and zinc were most likely the cause. I think this may be to improve our immune systems. Does someone have our backs? It was back to 'normal' two hours later. Weird at any time, but scary and to be expected in equal measure now. *It was this that prompted me to start keeping a diary on my Facebook page, as of yesterday (so to speak).*

I am now attempting Facebook isolation/lockdown. No posts or messaging - just this type of thing if there is anything interesting to report. This is my page. I don't expect many people at all to read it and I'm not looking for anyone to comment or like - it's a '*me*' thing for me. I have never kept a diary ordinarily, but these are extraordinary times. Please do feel free to copy this idea though. Think of it as a live art project! Big Brother might collate it for us! I would say 'stay safe' but I don't really know what that means any more! Stay sane might work better!

....

Variation on a Theme by Rilke by DENISE LEVERTOV
The Book of Hours, Book 1, Poem 1, Stanza 1

A certain day became a presence to me;
there it was, confronting me - a sky, air, light:
a being. And before it started to descend
From the height of noon, it leaned over
and struck my shoulder as if with
The flat of a sword, granting me
honor and a task. The day's blow
rang out, metallic or it was I, a bell awakened,
and what I heard was my whole self
Saying and singing what it knew: *I can.*

....

Allonby - Saturday, 28th March 2020

DAY 2

Monday 30th March 2020

Or at least that's what the laptop says it is. I do the '30 days hath September...' thing to check if it's one or two days to 1st April. I think I'll give April fooling a miss this year - people are believing anything.

I can still taste the 3 a.m. water - sickly sweet, cloying to the roof of my mouth. I would have sworn it was just me had I not had three attempts, from cupped hands, leaving the tap to run a little longer each time. Laura said I should ring the water company, but I couldn't be bothered to wait 5 hours for them to refuse to admit whether or not they were poisoning me. "We've all got better things to do with our time", I lie. I'm still alive (I think).

I made a purchase today: three poetry books that I'll probably never fully read - and one is 'mine' - well there's one poem of mine in it at least. They'll go on top of the ones I've never read from Birthday and Xmas, next to the pile of unplayed CDs I bought - but that *is* reducing.

I briefly flirt with trying to get the youngest to listen to Tangerine Dream, but all attempts are deemed futile - well it's *her* life that's not going to be changing, not mine! Talking of Tangerine Dream, I got a 'like' from their leader Thorsten for a comment I made below some potential album artwork I submitted, saying "I can still dream!". They're not too big or too busy these days to need to hire someone else to press the button - and there were no home computers in their 70s vinyl heydays anyway.

My cup is half full.

It's the small things.

I've stopped watching the news.

Tuesday is not expected to be as exciting.

Photos taken near Workington on 23/3/20, the day lockdown was introduced.

DAY 3

Day 3 of my diary. (31/3/20)

I awake, well rested. That makes a change these days, but I sleep like a log normally. I glance in the bathroom mirror to find Robinson Crusoe looking back at me. I am up earlier than I need to be, but my mind is awash with thoughts and I need to put them down.

I feed the cats. They seem the only ones who are ever really pleased to see me. I make a cup of tea and turn on BBC News. There's a piece about Police heavy-handedness. A short drive to find a safe, open space in which to walk your dog is now a serious crime it would seem, but I'm sure I heard a health expert recommending that last week.

I feel like a war diarist as I type - war poet would be too lofty an ambition. I don't know if the war has really started in earnest for most of us yet, but the enemy may be just outside our door. The four walls around us are our trenches. Hospitals are not the only front line, but they should be.

It's madness so many non-essential staff are still working - cannon-fodder to protect employers' profits, not just the economy. Not all heroes wear a uniform. There was one 'whistle-blower' on the BBC working for a sports clothing manufacturer.

We are all conscripts in a war not of our making. We are all on the same side. We should stop fighting among ourselves.

I wonder how many others are keeping a diary? Diaries are best kept private. They are a very private thing. I am stupid and brave in equal measure. But I worry more about people who live alone in these days of self-isolation. As someone who can feel lonely in a crowd I can empathise with them. I never feel lonely at home, but I know loneliness can be a killer. I hope my diary helps someone in some small way. It does help *me*.

I also worry about the many elderly folk (up to 99 years old!) and vulnerable people I have interviewed throughout the course of my job over the last seven and a half years or so. I hope they're all still doing well, but there will be many that aren't or that will, sadly, have passed away by the time this is over. I have met many people - too many - with mental health issues. I have met many people with respiratory conditions that will place them at very high risk - I did not realise how prevalent the lung disease COPD is in West Cumbria.

Cumbria has a disproportionate amount of old to young people than the national average. The number of elderly people in Cumbria is *way* above the national average. *I seem to recall reading that it was 23% higher.* This, coupled with the large number of people with respiratory problems, means we may (or will) be near the top of certain tables we will see. This is the reason - it's not that we aren't following guidelines. We should stop blaming people.

I pause this to make breakfast: poached eggs on toast. It's now 11 a.m. and no-one else has surfaced.

I wrote the poem that follows when I was a teenager. It was written for myself (and not for school). I sometimes use italics to show words that have been added to the diary dates later.

....

RISE AND SET

Dawn's egg cracks open and a fiery yolk is hatched

On a hazy skyline of grey-black chimney-pots.

It slowly rises, then soars -

An ocean of light flooding the dark void!

Nestling in cotton-wool clouds,

Distilling a gentle rain over eastern lands.

Migrating to the west coast, to be devoured

By the hungry beaks of crow-black cooling-towers.

....

The consensus is that there will be no family walk today - there was one "too tired", two who "can't be bothered" and me. That's two days in a row now. I may go out alone for a stroll later - without the car. I told you Tuesday wasn't going to be exciting.

There is a housing estate behind us nicknamed 'Bangla' - it's short for Bangladesh. You may be forgiven for thinking it means that there may be a lot of people of South Asian descent who live there. Give over! - this is Cumbria we're talking about. 'Bangla' is a derogatory term - due, I guess, to the poverty and deprivation traditionally associated with the area. The reality is it's nothing like Bangladesh, but a lot of people who live there do struggle. It's a mental health 'hotspot'. *I have no real evidence to back up that claim other than first hand experience of working in the area.* I quite like it. Some of the views from there are lovely. I blame the architects for it not looking as aesthetically pleasing as it otherwise might. It has an undeserved reputation picked up from years ago and, sadly, mud sticks sometimes! I speak as I find. People make a place and the vast majority of the ones I've met are lovely. I may go there for my walk and take some pictures.

A good friend contacts me from Bahrain to say that the name 'Bangla' came from the flat roofs originally put on to the houses when they were built. I think I knew this, but I didn't mention it. He says the comparison is neither fair on the country of Bangladesh or the housing estate. I feel the need to check with him that I hadn't been unkind, as this was not my intention - I was trying to be complimentary if anything. He reassures me that he was only complaining about it being given that 'nickname'.

In other news, we are being told that 'Panic Buying' is a mere 25% increase in sales over a 4-week period. The biggest increases - or the ones they seemed most keen to tell us about - were in alcohol and frozen goods. The fact that alcohol was mentioned in this gives me a warm glow and a reassurance that the British public always know when to get their priorities right!

That's all for today folks!

....

Up-Hill by CHRISTINA ROSSETTI

Does the road wind up-hill all the way?
    Yes, to the very end.
Will the day's journey take the whole long day?
    From morn to night, my friend.

But is there for the night a resting-place?
    A roof for when the slow dark hours begin.
May not the darkness hide it from my face?
    You cannot miss that inn.

Shall I meet other wayfarers at night?
    Those who have gone before.
Then must I knock, or call when just in sight?
    They will not keep you standing at that door.

Shall I find comfort, travel-sore and weak?
    Of labour you shall find the sum.
Will there be beds for me and all who seek?
    Yea, beds for all who come.

WORKINGTON - 23rd March 2020

Maryport night walk (top 3 photos) - 31/3/20 and near Flimby (bottom 3 photos) - 25/3/20.

DAY 4

03.38 - The water tastes fine.

It is Wed. 1st April - April Fool's Day.

I'm lying in bed, typing this in with my right thumb, in the dark. I switch to my left index finger until leaning on my elbow cuts off the circulation to my hand - it doesn't take long these days. Detail is going to be important today.

My body is still recovering from a 5k walk in the great outdoors I did with my step-son Ed last night - so much for a solo stroll! I had given him £20 earlier and I think he was repaying my kindness. He's a lovely lad! The sunset had been disappointing. Everywhere was deserted. Eerily quiet does not do it justice.

Warning: I will not be trying to pass off falsehood as truth today. We will be hearing enough fake news. But I think today might be a good day to share some dangerous information. So please look away if you are of a nervous disposition. But not now - laterzzzzzzzzzz!

....

I re-commence at 11.10.

I enjoyed being reminded, earlier, by my best mate - I don't have many! - of a football game in 1975 on a Tuesday night, 45 years ago to the day. Carlisle United beat Burnley 4-2 at Brunton Park in the old First Division. I can't remember a better game - and there have been many in my life. It was also memorable because I was so excited that I kissed my mate 'Ollie' *on the cheek* when the 4th goal went in! We were 13 years old. I can't remember much about the match details, but that moment stuck with me. It was uninhibited shared love of the game - the beautiful game!

It is difficult, in these times, to know whether people are posting stuff for 'April Fools' or whether they are just being fooled in April. Maybe others are thinking it's a good day for burying what they do believe to be true in a massive pile of other stuff that isn't. It's harder, generally, to tell the truth from the lies. The fog of war is definitely doing its trick!

Nicola Sturgeon is live on BBC News. I am very impressed with her - she is in a different league to Boris. It would take him all day and a couple of aides to deliver the information she is very competently presenting in Edinburgh, single-handedly. She is similarly competent in the Q&A's.

My family always keep me grounded. Laura just informed me that Ed is calling me Samuel Pepys. She prefers Anne Frank. I take them as compliments. I'm used to it. They take the piss out of me constantly!

....

I need to record some statistics for posterity. These are some mere 'snapshots' of the virus as it is currently, at this moment, frozen in time - no more or less. This reminds me of *Monty Python*'s 'Dead Parrot' sketch, but I must be serious.

The European death toll has just exceeded 30,000 people. It's important to remember these are people, not just a number. I'll predominantly limit other 'stats' to England and Wales or UK. The UK death toll stands at 1,808 people. (1,720 in England & Wales. Global death toll is 43,288 people). Figures at 13.02 p.m. 1/4/2020.

Now let us go back a few years.

EWM or EWD means excess winter mortality or deaths. In simple terms, it means how many *more* people die in the winter each year. What follows has been copied and pasted from the Office For National Statistics website (in their italics):

In England there were an estimated 21,900 excess winter deaths (EWD) in 2018 to 2019 with 46% among males (10,100 EWD) and 54% (11,800 EWD) among females. EWD are generally higher among females which may partly be explained by the higher proportion of females aged 90 years and over compared with males.

In comparison with the previous winter period, the EWM index in England has statistically significantly decreased for both sexes across all age groups. The largest percentage point differences between the winters of 2017 to 2018 and 2018 to 2019 were among those aged 90 years and over, with the females' index decreasing from 47.0% to 19.3% and males decreasing from 40.2% to 18.1%.

The highest EWM index during 2018 to 2019 was for males and females aged 90 years and over (18.1% and 19.3% respectively) which was statistically significantly higher than all other ages. Interestingly, the EWM index for males aged 85 to 89 years was statistically significantly lower than all years since the beginning of the time series in 1991 to 1992. In contrast, the EWM index for males aged 0 to 74 years was statistically significantly higher than winters 2015 to 2016 and 2016 to 2017 but was statistically significantly lower than 2017 to 2018.

In the 2017 to 2018 winter period, there were an estimated 50,100 excess winter deaths in England and Wales.
The number of excess winter deaths in 2017 to 2018 was the highest recorded since winter 1975 to 1976.

N.B. The bold highlighting above is my own - not that of the ONS.

During the winter months of 2017 to 2018, the number of daily deaths exceeded the daily five-year average for all days except 25 March.
Excess winter mortality in 2017 to 2018 significantly increased from 2016 to 2017 in all English regions and Wales, with Wales having the highest regional index.
Excess winter mortality continued to be highest in females and people aged 85 and over.
Excess winter mortality doubled among males aged 0 to 64 years between 2016 to 2017 and 2017 to 2018.

Over one-third (34.7%) of all excess winter deaths were caused by respiratory diseases.
<End>

Contains public sector information licensed under the Open Government Licence v3.0.
[Open Government Licence (nationalarchives.gov.uk)](http://nationalarchives.gov.uk)

The above ONS statistics are being provided by me at this stage to give perspective - not to promote complacency. It is vitally important to adhere to government guidelines. I will be continuing to self-isolate with my family. I will be washing my hands regularly, sticking to the two-metre rule when I go out for exercise etc.

I dropped the bold highlighted bombshell then chose to ignore it, but we'll come back to it!

I'm going to end here for today. I don't believe in a god, but I do say "may your God bless you all" if you do. Take care everybody! Peace and love to you all.

From 'Devotions Upon Emergent Occasions' by JOHN DONNE

No Man is an *Island*, entire of itself; every man is a piece of

The *Continent*, a part of the *main*; if a *Clod* be washed away

By the *Sea*, *Europe* is the less, as well as if a *Promontory* were,

Any Man's *death* diminishes *me*, because I am involved in

Mankind; And therefore never send to know for whom the

Bell tolls; It tolls for *thee*.

DAY 5

Day 5's Diary - simply these poems that we can all contribute to over the next week.

Friends PLEASE HELP by contributing your OWN POEMS in the comments below!

1st Prize

A £50 donation to your nominated charity!

Poems about Hope Overcoming Adversity

Light of Hope

When the chill of the night eats the fabric of your soul
And the clouds mask the moon and the fog it burns cold
And shelter is an unknown place beneath a blanket of trees,
Among peculiar animals, buried under dampened leaves,
Be assured that in some distant corner of the forest's gloom -
Even when all's against you - a candle burns for you.

HURDLER

I want to be a hurdler
To run in a hurdle race
To jump over every obstacle
That anyone can place
In my path - I'll take in stride
All before me - not collide
And never stumble over
Until the race is over!

An old photo originally shown in colour with the poem above overlaid onto it.

Facebook friends, please copy and paste your poems into the comments by 15th April. If you wish to participate anonymously, then please message me. Ideally, poems should be about Hope or Overcoming Adversity. If your poems are fairly short and I have a suitable photo of mine I can use, then I may be able to combine the two! The Winner will be announced on Thursday 16th April. Thank you!

I wrote this poem a very long time ago - decades ago. It has always seemed too dark and depressing to have shared before now. This poem's time has finally come at last. It contains a glimmer of hope in the final verse. My Poem: GREY, BLACK, SHADOW (see Page 16)

....

SOCKGATE by LAURA

Well, I've hunted high and low and I still can't find the socks!
The washing machine sits idle and quietly mocks.
"I've eaten them, I've eaten them, I've eaten all the socks!"
Not the uniforms, the shirts or the jeans,
Its hunger is for socks, and one of a pair it seems.
It has no preference for size or colour, my search of the drum is very thorough.
"I've eaten them, I've eaten them, I've eaten all the socks!"
I feed it daily and its appetite's tremendous.
My purchasing of new pairs appears to be endless!
My machine has become fussy, leaving the red wine stain,
But the insatiable need for socks appears to remain.
"I've eaten them, I've eaten them, I've eaten all the socks!"

N.B. There now follows an addition by me (as we took delivery of this type of machine!) which I'm not allowed to simply add on to the above!
Today we bought a new one, we've just taken it out of the box.
It's got a little extra door - just for feeding socks!
"Feed me socks! Feed me socks! Feed me socks!"
(The last line should be voiced in the style of a Dalek!)

2nd April - I had to go to the Post Office, so had a nice exercise walk - two birds and all that. I saw an older lady I've interviewed a few times - she now calls me a friend (as I do her) and was chuffed to bits to see me. She had a mask on, but I recognised the voice straight away. It was good to know that she and the elderly postmistress were alive and well.
When a police van was about to pass me for a *fourth* time during my walk, I had a speech prepared. I stuck out a thumb and the young PC waved back as he drove on by.
Little things mean a lot.

GREY, BLACK, SHADOW

These are dark, ordinary days.
Nothing stands out in their bleakness.
The world has failing sight,
But no-one will hold the torch
To lead it from this down-trodden path
To despair and self-destruction.
Night closes in fast on our twilight permanence,
But all lack the the urgency to deal with our predicament
And we stumble into darkness and we fall.

Out of the blackness
Eventually the sun will rise again,
But on my life and yours
No shadow will be cast.
No reminder of our insignificance
Will stain the pure brilliance
Of this bright new day.

STAY HOME! by LAURA

Don't stray too far, they said, stay inside!
Leave the car and commence the stride.
Only family - No. Large. Groups.
Then doorstep at 8 for claps and whoops.
The planes have been cancelled,
Your 'hols' are now history.
Chris Whitty and his team toil to solve the mystery.
Now any age, gender or class.
Every town, city, the deaths amass.
Don't go outside they say, be careful where you roam!
We will all get through this, if we all
Stay home!

DAY 6

My mum would have been 79 today. My granddad would have been about 108 I think.

<Facebook post - a black and white photo of mum and her dad on her wedding day> (See Page 18).

My late mother would have been 79 today. Her late husband - my step-dad - was 2 years younger than I am now when he died. I'm 58. I took this photo* to remind me of the dates they passed. My grandparents on my mother's side raised me. My dad died a long time ago. I don't remember him. *I was three years old when he died. He died a couple of months before my 4th birthday.* I could not find his gravestone on my last two trips to the cemetery. He committed suicide aged 28 *(after a failed earlier attempt)*. I don't really know why exactly. *I was told he would often sit in front of the fire and cry.* I've been meaning to ask again since I was first told of this 40 years ago. That was when my granddad died, a week before my 18th Birthday.

<*Facebook post - a photo of a memorial stone> (Not shown here)

I post this as part of Day 6 of my diary and to raise awareness of mental health issues. Few of us will not have had or not know someone who has had these. It is good to talk and show people they are not alone. I am not sad or unhappy today and my last memory of my mum is a very poignant and special one as she passed, but there are tears in my eyes as I type this.
I will keep that final moment private, but I was fortunate to share it with my brother, mum and step-dad's son. The three of us had never felt closer than in that beautiful moment.

I really feel for people who are now not able to say goodbye due to the pandemic and its social distancing.

Gill: Remember Castlerigg...?
Me: Close - it was Higham Hall. *(Note: The place where Gill, a 6th form school friend, and I were when I took the phone call advising me of my grandfather's death.)*
I do recall, however, a magical moment at Castlerigg - everyone lying on the floor of the meditation (?) room in the dark, listening to Mike Oldfield's *Tubular Bells*. Oh to be a teenage school student again!
Me: Gill, have you got any poems for my Hope and Overcoming Adversity project / competition?
Gill: I am not a poet...!

Pat: I can remember your dad he was a good looking man - best person to ask about him is Aunty Anne and Uncle Brian, I think Aunty Anne would be the best one, she might know where he is buried xxx

Cousin Linda W. offers to point out the location of my father's grave.

I dedicate this page to my grand-parents, Olive and Jack Scott, who raised me until adult-hood. I could sometimes be 'difficult' and you deserved much better. I never really knew my dad, but I do love and miss all these folks that I did get to know - as well as others who are not pictured here.

From top left, clockwise: Me; me; mum and her dad - my granddad Jack; my dad and mum; my mum and my step-dad Jim; my mum's mum - my nanna Olive. Photographer bottom left is me, the rest are unknown.

DAY 7

Saturday 4th April 2020

I awoke with a start from my dream around 8 a.m. Government health officials - middle-aged women in unfashionable garb and looking prim in their spectacles - were forcibly removing children from their parents during a pandemic.

My schedule is relaxed today. It will mainly consist of doing very little - similar to the rest of the week. I must confess I never get bored and I never struggle to fill these otherwise empty days with something. The days still seem to pass quickly - something that comes as you get older, I think. It must be more difficult for those who lack the internet, I assume - possibly wrongly.

BBC News channel informs us that Sir Keir Starmer is new leader of the Labour Party. Whilst I am pleased that they've chosen the best candidate, in my opinion, I care very little about party politics at this time. It's about as interesting or as meaningful to me today as a virtual Grand National would be!

I am continuing to invite contributions to my competition/personal project: Poetry Of Hope: Overcoming Adversity (or similar title!). The Great North Air Ambulance Service (GNAA) has already benefited from donations of £40 so far and the winner will receive a £50 donation, paid by myself, to a charity of their choice. It is perfectly fine to contribute a poem and not make a donation.

Now for a bit of a recap of the last few days:

Thursday gave me the idea of trying to solicit some poems from my Facebook friends and Laura!

Laura, to my amazement, produced 2 great little poems in no time! I managed to get out for exercise (via the Post Office) and took some photos down by the sea, sticking some of the better ones up on Facebook as usual.

I decided to use the idea of getting through this pandemic with the help of words to raise funds for charity. I initially made a payment of £25 (in lieu of a 2nd Prize) to GNAA, before deciding to set up a fund-raising Target of £250 where people could donate. The current total stands at £15. If all goes to plan I will nominate a 1st Prize Winner and make a further donation of £50 to a registered charity of their choice. In addition, I will nominate a 2nd Prize Winner who will receive a modest prize of a recent poetry compilation - no prizes for guessing which one!

I hope one day to maybe get someone to publish this diary, together with the collection of poetry and a few of my photographs. If successful, all poetry contributors will each receive a free copy. At worst, two charities will have got a total of at least £90 and only my ego will have taken a light bruising!

Most of the rest of the time has been spent enjoying banter with my lovely Laura. We've been pretending to be in Madeira on holiday - that's where we should have been now - and have been playing caricatures of our 'holiday selves' in Welsh, Irish and Cockney accents! We'd go down a storm on Gogglebox!

As a result of posting some deeply personal stuff yesterday (3rd April) to raise awareness of suicide and mental health issues, I am delighted to say a cousin has come forward to help me find my late father's grave. Thank you Linda! Yesterday was a far more emotional 3rd April than usual - but it seems harder to bury one's feelings when there's nothing else going on in which to submerge yourself.

This is the end of Week 1 of keeping this online diary. I started this project as a diversion, perhaps a coping mechanism, to help me reduce the 20 hours per day (or so it seemed) researching and privately discussing this virus with a few of you. Researching and discussing the relative merits of all the different conspiracy theories, the flu vaccine - who gets it and its production process, EWD statistics and mortality rates etc. did take its toll. Things were getting a bit much for me and, whilst I learnt a lot and there were, what I thought, genuine 'eureka!' moments, it was all raising more questions than answers and I realised there was absolutely nothing I could do about the current situation in which we and the rest of the World now find ourselves. What's done is done. We are where we are.

I've decided to let go of this frustration now. I'm enjoying keeping this diary, listening to music, doing my poetry thing and my photography stuff, but the research must now stop. I've managed to reduce my hours online by half. I'm feeling a lot better and well rested. I will be keeping this diary private from now on. I will still post my photos on the odd occasion I'm out and about and may still post the odd comment. If anyone has been reading these (online) posts, then I thank you for putting up with me and my crazy ramblings. I dearly hope you and your families get through this. See you on the other side!

MARYPORT 2/4/20

DAY 8

Sunday 5th April 2020

A week after I started my online (Facebook) diary it is now a private diary - recorded in a 'day per file' format stored on my laptop computer.

I have decided to do this for two reasons: firstly, self-doubt. I am doubting the value of making my journal public. I don't want to become an annoyance or a figure of ridicule. I may be both, I may be neither. I have no idea. Secondly, I do not want to be inhibited - I want to speak freely, I want to let myself go, I don't want to have to speak in measured language simply to avoid upsetting people or to appear not to be going against the popular line - however slim the chances of that may be.

I got up a bit later than of late. "Later than of late" gave 4 results in 0.57 seconds on Google.

I dream a lot during sleep - Laura would say I'm very much a dreamer in real life anyway. I just checked this with her and she said "very much so". That gives me a mild sense of satisfaction, but I stopped short of giving her my smuggest 'look'. My dreams tend to have a pandemic theme running throughout them now - last night these were linked to my former career working as a Brewery Representative.

Today will be a day of random reflection I think. I think of all the care workers I've met in almost eight years of interviewing - that's a hell of a job at any time, but now? I send a generic message of love to them over a public Facebook post. I put up a link to a favourite TD track - 'Sensing Elements' to 'kick-start' Sunday and hope it turns on a few people enough to want to listen to the full 13 minutes or so. These may be the only posts I make today.

My engagements with BBC News are infrequent now. I am pleased we are hearing about the plight of care homes and care workers - it's not just the NHS workers who are faced with extremely difficult workplaces and extremely difficult choices at this time. The Health Secretary is threatening to remove the right for us to go out for daily exercise due to a few people sun-bathing in a park. I think it's a hollow threat, it'd better be. Exercise in the fresh air helps the body's immune system fight off viruses.

Spain's Covid death numbers reducing three days in a row, the Premier League Footballer pay cuts dispute and an 'exit strategy' formulated in the next week or so get a mention. We hear two advance excerpts from The Queen's Speech which is due later tonight. They are at great pains to tell us that social distancing rules have been followed - I didn't realise that it was *that* easy to get near the Queen anyway!

Well within the time that it took me to think of and type this, Laura wrote and handed me the poem on the next page. She followed that one up with a poem of pure filth, voiced in the style of Her Majesty no less, and depicting an act - we'll leave it at that - between her and her husband, Prince Philip - Duke of Edinburgh. I'm sure this constitutes an act of treason, but we'll gloss over that. It's amazing what we get up to, to amuse ourselves and pass the time, in these days of 'opening up' and letting our hair down behind closed doors, away from public scrutiny. We are often at our funniest in times of adversity and uncertainty.

....

CRAIG by LAURA

Your hair grows wilder with each passing day.
Sometimes unshaven, but that too is okay.
You sit in your shorts, socks and slippers.
As time passes, I will wish I owned some clippers!
I love you regardless, I love you cos you're you!

You awoke as Irish and then became a Scot.
Later you'll be Welsh or a pirate - we'll have the lot.
In the position, computer perched on lap,
Fingers moving quickly with the tap, tap, tap.
I love you regardless, I love you cos you're you!

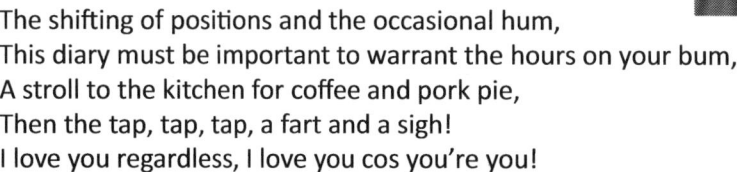

The shifting of positions and the occasional hum,
This diary must be important to warrant the hours on your bum,
A stroll to the kitchen for coffee and pork pie,
Then the tap, tap, tap, a fart and a sigh!
I love you regardless, I love you cos you're you!

You embrace each venture with gusto and pride.
There's no place I'd rather be than by your side.
Each day you make me giggle and sometimes cry with laughter.
That's why we'll have a happily ever after!
I love you regardless, I love you cos you're you!

....

I have been in silly, dressing-up mode - posting a 'bad taste' picture of myself in silly hat, sunglasses and face mask on Facebook - but adding a good message to redeem myself, ever so slightly. I imagine wearing similar garb and videoing myself either singing or reading out her poem about me in an alien accent, not one of my own, but I manage to resist temptation - for now. I ask Laura if she's got anything that we can make into a makeshift crown - she can tell where this one is going and makes a hasty retreat! Instead I make a short video of myself, as newly-created character Welsh Stevie, reaching out to his friends across the globe, in places as diverse as Aberystwyth, Paris and Pontypandy: "Stay at home, stay safe and God bless".

....

Ed went out for a bike ride this morning. He went out again later to the local Tesco Express and, on his return, left some flowers on his girlfriend's doorstep - together with a cake he had baked for her. He's the only one who's been out of the house in the last two days.

It's difficult to gauge how the rest of Cumbria is getting on. I only tend to listen to BBC Radio Cumbria when I'm in the car. A lot of people are making out there's one big party going on. They're well stocked where alcohol is concerned and online get-togethers are being arranged - with music, karaoke, fancy dress, quizzes etc. I've had invites and reminders, but I enjoy my own company and that of Laura and the time passes relatively quickly without the need for outside intervention.

I wonder how the lonely people are getting on; the people who live on their own; those who have no relatives, no-one who cares about them in their lives; those who lack the confidence to even participate in online get-togethers. The anonymous without a face. The faceless Facebookers who merely observe and don't interact with anyone - save for a very few trusted 'friends' or no-one. I hope someone is looking out for those people right now.

Then there's the jokes and the jokers. Never have so many jokes been distributed by so many in such a short period of time. These are a well-meaning diversion, but I suppose they can occasionally become slightly tiresome to some when you've read two or three versions of the same joke for the 2nd or 3rd time. In some ways it's good that people can still laugh in the face of adversity; people can still be bothered to put on a brave face; people can still rally the troops for the doorstep claps and whoops! But I do wonder for how long it might last before the boredom sets in. Are these the internet equivalent of burying one's head in the sand? I wonder what will happen if the lockdown is extended - rather than relaxed a bit - and we've still got a while to go before that will be decided.

I wonder how long it will be before we'll all have been touched by the death of a relative, a neighbour or someone we know in our area - or worse! What will we all do then?
The news filters through that our Prime Minister, Boris Johnson, has been admitted to hospital for tests. The PM continues to have persistent symptoms of coronavirus ten days after testing positive for the virus, says No.10. I hope Boris gets some rest and recovers fully, maybe delaying his return until all of this is over.

My last entry for the day records some of the deaths from Coronavirus (Covid-19) per 1 Million population as follows:-

China - 2 (TWO!!!), UK - 73, Italy - 263 (2nd highest globally), Spain - 268 (Highest globally).

Total deaths from the virus globally stand at 69,177. UK deaths are 4,934 of that total.

(Source: Worldometer)

....

'The (C)rude Awakening: Citizen F Life Cycle / Expectancy' - 2022

Photos on Pages 24 & 25 were taken in Maryport on Thursday, 2nd April 2020

DAY 9

Monday 6th April 2020

'Apartment Machico near the beach' - that's the property where Laura and I would have been travelling to today, the third place we had booked to stay at whilst on holiday in Madeira. It would have been two weeks in a place and country - it belongs to Portugal - we had never previously visited (and still haven't). It seems somewhat trivial to mention it now, but it is a fact nonetheless. I wonder how the sand would be feeling between my toes right now? I can almost hear the waves crashing and smell the salt air.

Apart from the routine of cooking (which we share between 3 of us) and washing-up (which is almost exclusively done by me), there is the ritual of catching up on news headlines - little much else than headlines by now. I took advantage earlier of something called 'Notepad' on my budget android smart-phone, to make a few hand-written notes. I am starting to elaborate on them for this diary - that's the other daily ritual. Anything else is a bonus, a surprise, something unexpected.

I will aim to try to catch up with more relatives this week over the phone. It was great to catch up with my brother last week. He, sadly, was made redundant in January - before this all started in the UK - following the closure of the depot where he worked. I also caught up with a 70-year old cousin of my late mum. A lovely, kind and gentle lady who informed me she has a mobile home near Stranraer. Her 74 year old husband tows his boat to and from there and enjoys solitary fishing trips. I am not a fisherman, but I dropped a hint and welcomed an invitation to try out the facilities, both on land and out at sea. I think we were both using lure and bait and I await the 'catch' when all this is over.

Laura has been furloughed from her job as a receptionist in a leisure centre, but she is on holiday at the moment. I expect to be the same, but I work few hours these days anyway. It was a relief when I received a small payment on 3rd April for my work in March, but I am uncertain as to what I will receive going forward. Thankfully work is not my only source of income these days, but it is a bit of a struggle financially. I decided to 'sort out' my pensions and semi-retire following a short, but serious bout of illness about 2 years ago. I survived bacterial and viral meningitis and sepsis. Thanks to a strong heart, the love of a wife who was by my side daily and the NHS doctors and nurses at West Cumberland Hospital, Whitehaven - thank you all! - I came through it. I was one of the lucky ones. I doubt I'll be as lucky ever again. Having said that, I won't be able to afford to live long without more work income!

The news informs us that the Chief Medical Officer for Scotland has resigned following criticism of her choice to drive from Edinburgh to a second home she has in Fife on, I believe, two occasions. I thought this was a relatively short journey, but they claim it's over an hour away. Despite taking every precaution to limit the risk involved, it was a very bad career choice and it sets a bad example to others, but I do have some sympathy.

We hear that calls to domestic abuse helplines are up by 25%. As someone who has experience of this in a previous relationship, I do worry about those who have to share a confined space for up to 24 hours a day with someone who could violently erupt at any time. I imagine it might also cause problems where previously there had never been any, but that is not to excuse it. This is an issue usually, but not exclusively, where women are the victims.

Women also fare badly in the latest analysis done by the Institute for Fiscal Studies, reports *The Guardian*. The low-paid, young people and women are likely to be the hardest hit by the shutting down of businesses - restaurants, hotels, pubs, retailers and transport services. It states that low earners are seven times more likely as high earners to work in a business sector that has shut down. Analysis by the IFS found a third of the bottom 10% of earners worked in the worst-hit sectors, against one in 20 of those who worked in the top 10%. Women were about one-third more likely than men to work in a sector that has been shut down, as they make up the bulk of retail and hospitality workers.

I imagine it is unbelievably tough at the moment if you're a young woman with a low income who has been working in one of those sectors until very recently.

We also hear the news that Boris has had to be moved into an Intensive Care Unit.

I do wish him a speedy recovery - much as I dislike his *modus operandi*.

Finally, I regret to inform you of the death of a bee. Laura brought it into the house last night in a pile of washing. I managed to locate the item it had attached itself to, but when I shook it out it flew up into the light shade, instead of down into a pinch of sugar and a few drops of water on a spoon. I opened the back door and left the spoon nearby to try to coax it out. We thought it had got out, but we discovered it still in the light shade this morning.

A dead bee.

A little hope extinguished.

....

Excerpt from 'Auguries of Innocence' by WILLIAM BLAKE

To see a World in a Grain of Sand

And a Heaven in a Wild Flower,

Hold Infinity in the palm of your hand

And Eternity in an hour.

....

DAY 10

I was up before 9 a.m. and had three poached eggs on three slices of toasted wholemeal bread. I also had a cup of tea, of course, with milk and two sugars added. I think today will be a slow news day so you may see more totally unnecessary, irrelevant detail than normal! I also add a pinch of salt, as usual!

We have had no wi-fi since late last night. Ironically, the family had been discussing having one day per week where we all went without the internet. Laura went against this idea and we decided that that should be an individual choice - not an imposed one. It now looks like that has been taken out of our hands. My mobile phone and mobile data come to the rescue.

A friend has shared someone else's post showing a video. A "self-entitled" lady videos herself being arrested by two police officers after 'exercising her mind' on a bench, well away from others, by a river. She was wanting to stay there until the sun had set. There are no comments, but the original post's comments were mixed. I wonder why Boris has not been chastised for continually failing to social-distance in the early stages of the virus and ending up in his current predicament, but I did not dare ask this in the comments.

My News Feed goes berserk with 'Clap For Boris' posts. A friend has joined a Facebook Group of this name - and there's more than one it seems - and invited me to do so. I politely decline, but not before I am inundated with posts to the site. Eventually I find a way to rid myself of these and post "Get in there!!!!!" - explaining my little 'joke'. *No joke!* 'Clap For Boris' is scheduled for 8 p.m. tonight. I won't be participating, but I do wish him a speedy recovery and hope he gets the clap he deserves!

A postman plays 'knock and nash'. I feel a flush of excitement seeing three parcels - one through the letter-box and two that were left on the door-step. I am like a soldier stationed abroad receiving parcels from home. The poetry books I ordered have come a day early -

including the one to which I have contributed. The kids have a parcel each too - a CD for Beth and a charging block for Ed's mobile phone.

It later transpires that the lack of internet is associated with the theft of some 600 metres of copper wire! The police are involved. *I was slow to notice the pun.* The internet was down for over 20 hours. All 4 of us survived relatively unscathed!

'Clap For Boris' came and went. We didn't hear a peep.

Laura and I spend most of the evening listening to a recording of **DAVID ICKE - THE CORONAVIRUS CONSPIRACY: HOW COVID-19 WILL SEIZE YOUR RIGHTS & DESTROY OUR ECONOMY** on London Real. It was broadcast live yesterday (6/4/20). It was very interesting and very profound. Some of it was very believable - echoing my own thoughts about Covid-19 reporting and testing. Some of it was very controversial and a bit of a stretch.

Laura agrees.

I fell out somewhat with David Icke over Brexit and The General Election, but he is on overdrive at the moment and back to his best conspiracy theory form.

He may not be the Son of God, but he is a very naughty boy and a lot of his prophesies appear to be coming to fruition right now.

Right here. Right now

Photos on Pages 28-30 were taken in Maryport on Wednesday, 8th April 2020

DAY 11

06.37 A.M. *(8/4/20)*

I am watching BBC 1 'Breakfast'. I have had a mildly restless night, but I do not feel overly tired. I have already fed the cats and washed last night's supper dishes - Ed made sweet 'n' sour chicken, the ladies did their own thing. Beth, the veggie, had oven chips with curry sauce. I do hope she's eating healthily overall and mentioned this to her mum last night. She reminded me that she ate cabbage with her tea the night before, so all is well. I drink a cup of tea and just try to take all this - the pandemic - in for a moment. There is a mature lady doing exercises with her feet tucked under a sofa - a blast from the past, it's the Green Goddess.

I did toy earlier with the idea of going out and trying to photograph (during a potential exercise walk) the setting of the Supermoon. There was a fair bit of cloud around, looking through the windows, and the setting location in the South-West was not going to be a favourable one. I quickly abandoned the idea.

The Mayor of London, Sadiq Khan, is stressing the importance of social-distancing and obeying the rules when doing exercise in parks. We learn that Paris is to ban exercise during daylight hours to avoid daytime congestion. 'The Special One', Jose Mourhinho, is being criticised for taking a training session in a park.

I check Worldometer. Its coronavirus statistics show that 10.5 people per 1 Million population have died from the virus world-wide. This will rise - only time will tell us by how much or how little. The UK figure is 91 per 1 Million people. I wonder if there had been a tipping-point figure in mind when our strategy was first laid out on the table, like a battlefield of toy soldiers, before the first casualties fell or, perhaps, seconds after the first imaginary cannons were fired.

Boris Johnson is said to be in a stable condition. We are told that lockdown is unlikely to be reviewed any time soon.

I am looking forward to the coming-together of two poetry groups tonight: 'SpeakEasy' (Carlisle) meets 'Poets Out Loud' (Cockermouth) for an online get-together. I have not written anything special for it. I juggle with the ideas of reading poems written by others that are appropriate to our current predicament, reading old poems of my own that I've not read before and reading suitable entries from my diary. I may do a combination of two or three - depending on how many people are participating and how many 'rounds' we can accommodate.

There's a gentleman on TV who has just left hospital after 12 days there being gravely ill with coronavirus. He revels in telling us how much joy he got - and how much his emotions overcame him - from the simple pleasure of a nurse kindly giving him a long overdue shave to the nurses who brought him a birthday cake and sang for him. Sadly, he lost his father whilst he was hospitalised and tells us that none of the family were able to be at the funeral, unfortunately, because they were all self-isolating. But they were at least able to watch some footage of it online.

I check my Gmail - it's thin on the ground of late. I'm lucky, I never get much spam. There's confirmation from Easyjet that our flight cancellation refunds have finally been processed. I have received refunds (or a voucher alternative) for everything apart from one accommodation booking - 'Sod's Law', it's the most expensive of the three. I do not know if this is going to re-scheduled free of charge to 2021 or if the money is simply lost now - my emails from a few weeks ago continue to be ignored. I type a cheap line about a planned holiday to Madeira being no piece of cake.

The Guardian introduces me to a little mammal called a pangolin - I had never heard of these before. The pangolin may be a link between bats and humans in terms of the virus. They are scaly anteaters with (expectedly) long tongues that eat up ants. They have protective keratin scales covering their skin.

I decide to go back to bed for a few hours and snuggle into Laura until she can no longer bear the heat from my body or the weight of my leg on top of hers and I turn over. Laura had to switch on the fan beside her bed in the early hours - it is getting warmer, but I can't tell the difference. I sleep for two hours until a dream awakens me - Beth has been trashing the bathroom, the sink is no longer there, secured to the wall below the window; all the tiles have been removed from the walls - it is like a blank canvas. I drift off to sleep again. The bedroom window is ajar, there is the occasional bark of a neighbour's dog or a cock crowing and the metal on wood noise of next door's garden gate opening and closing. I wake for the final time just after 11 a.m.

I have my own black dog for company now. I feel like shit. Most of my minor ailments compete for attention: my pulsating tinnitus in my left ear is as loud as ever; my eyes drift lazily out of sync; my good right (not replaced) hip is aching; my throat is dry and burning slightly; my hands are numbest, my feet not far behind - a sign of my pre-diabetes status or is it the full-blown thing? I am in remission from my SUNCT (headache syndrome) currently, so my right knee pain is the only thing suspicious by its absence - perhaps a sign of how many days since I last left the house. I'm low in confidence and self-esteem for no apparent reason other than the above. That makes me a little annoyed with myself and I worry that I may have to miss tonight's online poetry session.

Brunch needs to be a good one full of restorative qualities. Baked beans on wholemeal toast and the prospect of taking a walk with Laura later lifts my spirits. The longer I fail to do something, the harder it is to do these days. I went to 'Poets Out Loud' in December. I last left the house for a walk on...well, let this Facebook post tell you:
I'm hoping to go out for a walk later - I will be taking the car (and a camera) and combining it with a shopping trip. It will only be my 2nd trip out of the house since Thursday last week and my first exercise walk since then. Do I qualify for some sort of a medal or do I have to sit on the naughty step when I get back? (followed by 3 'cod-eyed' laughing emojis) <end>
Although I consider myself shy and reserved by nature, I do have an exhibitionist side. I can be articulate and confident sometimes but, on the whole, I have reverted to type. I am not the man I was two years ago, before I became seriously ill. My exhibitionist side has been relatively untested since then, but today showing face in the outdoors seems testing enough.

I need not have worried. It was a breeze. Laura and I enjoy a lovely walk on the pebbles down by the sea and back along the cliff top and the harbour wall. I take lots of photos until the battery dies on my Nikon compact - not to worry, we were nearly done.

We stop at the local mini-market and Laura does some light shopping - it includes some beers for me, some chocolate treats for the kids, bread, milk, a few other essentials and some stuff for tea. Laura makes a mean spicy bolognese sauce with pasta later. Beth has veggie sausages, the rest of us have mince. Laura and I enjoy a glass of red from the bottle to which she treated herself and we all partake of the garlic bread as if it is our last supper.

I enjoy a couple of beers and the online company of some lovely poetry people later - despite having low bandwidth for much of the time. The rest of the family kindly came off the internet to help somewhat and an enjoyable couple of hours quickly pass. I manage to fit in four poems written by Mr & Mrs F from Maryport - two each.

Photos on Pages 32-33 were taken on 8th April 2020

DAY 12

Today was Friday, last night, when I set my alarm *and* when it woke me up this morning, at 07.15, in time to put the bins out. Two bins today - green and black. Friday is bin day in Maryport and this Friday, despite being Good Friday, will be 'business as usual'. Next week's black bin will be collected on Saturday 18th April - a day later than usual. It was Friday when I dragged two full bins down 15 steep steps and put them in the lane. It was still Friday when I noticed that everyone else must have forgotten to do the same. I double-check to confirm again that the bins were being collected on Friday 10th April. It was *still* Friday when I put a post on Facebook to remind people of this - just in case they thought they would be getting collected on Saturday 11th instead.

Then I noticed it wasn't Friday 10th April at all - it was Thursday 9th. It wasn't Good Friday until tomorrow - it wasn't even a Friday at all! - and it certainly wasn't a good start to a common or garden Thursday! So I decide to go back to bed and just stay there for as long as I can get away with it, hoping no-one noticed the post before I deleted it!

I eventually get up about noon. I pass the time with the usual stuff. Laura and Beth go out to do a 'big shop' in Workington, about 6 miles away. I check my Gmail and receive confirmation that I have been furloughed on 80% of (a minimum of) average pay for 2019-20. That's better than I had been anticipating - I sign and agree to this straight away.

BBC News has some report about 'raving Mancs' or something - there's a map with lots of coloured spots, denoting house and street parties etc. They are gatherings that breach lockdown regulations. The figures are staggering! Party *not* on!

There's disastrous news that the organ transplant system may be about to collapse.

Elsewhere, farmers are dumping milk due to a lack of demand from the hospitality industry and some may go out of business before demand increases. It is not having as much of an impact on farms who supply supermarkets. Cows are still producing milk we are told.

We switch to Moscow and hear of Russian cosmonauts who have left quarantine to orbit the earth. Closer to home, a Facebook 'local radio celebrity' friend reports that a Swaledale sheep has been exposed by low water, resting in the fork of a tree. The prognosis is not good - the floods were weeks ago.

Laura and I enjoy a video call on WhatsApp with her eldest daughter, her fiance and their little dog. There is much banter and laughter galore. Towards the end of it, something flashes up to say that Prime Minister, Boris Johnson, has been moved out of intensive care. To where I do not know.

Beth comes downstairs - that's an event in itself these days! - near-hysterical and fending off the tears. She has locked herself out of her eBay account and has tried every which way to get in, to no avail. She has tried every previous incarnation and password she can remember.

She has an 'Item Not As Described case' open with a seller and the seller has been messaging her 'off piste', trying to avoid the system. Worse than that, an item she has bid on is ending in less than 24 hours and she's the highest bidder at 99p or some similar small amount! Woe is me! I manage to get her calmed down and she sits next to me as we calmly adopt a systematic approach using logic and lateral thinking and eventually reach a positive solution. She's now back at the point before she lost it! It's worth all the time and effort (and even the tantrum!) to get a big 'thank you' cuddle as I kiss her on the cheek. She spends the next happy hour snuggling in and chatting.

All is well in our world again!

....

'MY HEART LEAPS UP WHEN I BEHOLD' by WILLIAM WORDSWORTH

My heart leaps up when I behold

    A Rainbow in the sky:

So was it when my life began;

So is it now I am Man;

So be it when I shall grow old,

    Or let me die!

The Child is Father of the Man;

And I could wish my days to be

Bound each to each by natural piety.

'Cat Values'
Ink Drawing
2022

DAY 13

Deja Vu! (10/4/20)

I get up early, making sure both large refuse receptacles are in place before the collectors come round. 'Key Workers' dutifully serve them up to RCVs who gobble up their contents and clank their appreciation.

I quickly notice three posts from friends across the globe. They inspire me to write the following three Hay(na)ku - variations on a Haiku - an idea for today started by a friend of a friend:

Slow
One for
Crucifying a Filipino?*

Friends
In Bahrain
Must wear masks

Aussies
Hopping mad
About the lockdown

The three above are based on friends' posts that I woke up to, but I write two further ones (below). To save space here, I have decided that the first line/word can double as the title of each of the five!

Swaledale
In tree
Low water exposes

(A sad one based on a post I mentioned yesterday.)

Collectors
Have emptied
Two plastic receptacles

(A 'thumbs up' to Good Friday key workers!)

*Apparently it's a tradition in The Philippines on Good Friday for some devout Christians to volunteer to be crucified as part of the local observance of Holy Week. Related practices include carrying wooden crosses, self-flagellation and crawling over rough ground.
This 'mortification of the flesh' enables one to beg forgiveness for former sins or to express gratitude for favours granted.

We hear that Boris Johnson is now on a ward and it is said that he is in good spirits.

I spent some time washing up, cleaning the cooker, putting away and generally hanging round in the kitchen, to the sound of music. I am now equipped with enough technical ability to be *au fait* on my own with Alexa - a friend of Laura. I have previously only enjoyed a couple of brief, supervised encounters with her. Today we did a little heavy petting to Led Zeppelin and Yes.

I can't wait to get more intimate next time.

Covid-19 is looking to be very much a bigger problem in Western Europe (and New York) than anywhere else right now.

Coronavirus deaths per 1 Million population:
World - 12.5
Switzerland - 114
UK - 118
Netherlands - 147
France - 187
Belgium - 260
Italy - 302
Andorra - 337 (low population, only 26 deaths)
Spain - 339
San Marino - 1,002 (low population, only 34 deaths)
Source: Worldometer - 16.20 10/4/20

DAY 14

Saturday, 11th April

I awake when 'Shouty Woman' from over the way bellows at her dogs, from behind her garden gate, to come home after their daily morning shit on the grass bank.

I type this as I eat three buttered toasted crumpets and drink my tea. I'm feeling a bit grumpy. You might want to skip this page and the next (should there be one) and go to Sunday. Laura says you might want to skip this 'whateveritis' altogether - at least that's what I think she would say if she wasn't too busy ignoring me!

Ed has come downstairs to quickly demolish whatever it is he has made himself for breakfast. He quickly demolishes everything he eats - he once binge-watched Man V. Food and now it seems to be his mission in life to minimise the amount of time any food spends on a plate - anywhere and at any time. His mere presence in the room irritates me. He looks like a young Adonis. He is toned and muscular. His curly hair looks better for being a bit longer than he would like. His complexion is darker these days - it's tanned from long bike rides and jogs on his exercise trips out. He mumbles some nonsense about how it would be possible to install a pull-up bar in his bedroom if it was re-arranged in a certain configuration - although, he says, he knows his mum would never allow it. This from a young man who doesn't know the meaning of the words "tidy up your room" or "put your bike away" or "clean up after yourself" or "leave things as you find them" or whatever follows the phrase "please make sure you remember to..."! His mum tells him to fuck right off - exactly what I was thinking, except she didn't use the 'F word' or any of those words, actually.

The little girl who lives in the small bedroom - I seldom see her and forget her name! - has failed to surface yet, but it is still this side of the afternoon after all.

I spend most of the day standardising my diary entries thus far - tidying up, proof-reading and sense-checking in the process. I fill the odd empty space on a page with an appropriate poem to catch or match, as best as I can, the mood of the page.

The daily Coronavirus press conference features a change of personnel. We have the Home Secretary, Priti Patel, making an appearance. She is well-prepared. I'd say cold and calculating if I wish to be harsh. She drops the requisite 'key' words and phrases into parts of her address and Q&A's that are likely to be the oft-played soundbites, but makes a huge gaffe. It is the sort of career-destroying error - or at least a fatal blow to one's political ambitions - that would not have appeared to have been ignored so readily by the BBC or dismissed (as it is likely to be) by the right-wing press had it been made by a black, female Labour politician with the initials D.A.

Ed - my wonderful step-son - makes a most delicious sweet 'n' sour chicken supper. It is quite possibly the best I've ever had. It is sweet and I am no longer sour!

DAY 15

Sunday 12th April 2020

Easter Sunday

Pope Francis has just given his dead-pan Easter message to the World in a near-deserted Basilica of Saint Paul at the Vatican on BBC1. It is refreshing to hear that he is not simply just focussing on the pandemic and mentions quite a few conflicts of which vast numbers of the public (myself included) will be unaware. I'm an atheist, but he is still a very relevant figure in many millions of people's lives.

The speech and the reading of the pre-written translation of it, to be fair, are both delivered in dull-as-dishwater tones. I do not get the impression this is merely to reflect a pious sobriety. I do not know if this is due to old age and fragility or the sheer enormity of the task of having to be leader of a World-wide religion at a time of global crisis. But, it seems to me, it is as if the person delivering the speech is totally detached from it, totally devoid of emotion and lacking any passion for any cause contained within it. This annual ritual is rarely any different from the usual it seems - despite the extraordinary circumstances in which the world currently finds itself.

News comes through that Boris Johnson has now left hospital and is to continue his recovery at Chequers, his official country residence. I really do not care how long it takes him to come back to work. I hope he takes as long as necessary to fully recover, but I am somewhat amazed later to find him making a public announcement that appears to be live to camera. It is almost as if he wishes to create the impression that *his* recovery is as remarkable and significant as that of a certain Christian martyr over two thousand years ago.

I may be an atheist, but if Jesus Christ *did* exist - and I make no claim of denial - then he would definitely be one of my heroes. I wonder what his social media posts would be looking like today. I'm sure he'd be kicking off, in one way or another, big time!

Earlier I made private this post, one that I had made public on Facebook a few hours earlier this morning:

"I will only leave this here for a short period of time or until Facebook removes it.
We all need to stop doing chain letter style posts designed to flood our news feeds and bury discussion about what is really going on in hospitals etc, because the few images on our TV screens and computers we are seeing do not suggest the pandemic is quite what we are being told it is.

Yes, we are being told there are lots of people dying each day *with* (not *from*) Coronavirus, but the figures are not that meaningful without knowing total deaths (from any cause) each day. The Coronavirus 'death' figures are below the number of deaths you normally get each day in the UK.

We do need more brave NHS workers to break their vows of silence, but I have read posts from critical care nurses saying ICU Departments are less busy than usual or eerily quiet. We have seen hospital corridors full of staff standing round clapping a survivor leaving the premises; we have staff grouped together, ignoring social distancing, making videos. We have lines of police vehicles and ambulances standing idle outside hospitals etc."

That post was borne out of frustration. I'm not intending to have a go at NHS staff. It's just that the visual narrative we are seeing is not matching the headline figures we are being given by the mainstream media. The staff do not appear to be running around like war-time medics, they appear to have a fair bit of time on their hands. I could be totally wrong, but my brain can only compute with the visual information my eyes are receiving. It can understand the negative spin the media give to the Covid-19 death figures, but it can temper this with the sense of perspective that the ranking in 'death per 1M population' Worldometer figures allows us to make. The more sources of information our brains can receive, the better we can understand the nature and impact of this virus. This allows us to formulate our own opinions and lets us draw our own informed conclusions - not just have us believe what the mainstream media would have us believe.

Coronavirus deaths per 1 Million population:

World - 14.1
Switzerland - 120
UK - 145
Netherlands - 154
France - 212
Belgium - 311
Italy - 322
Andorra - 337 (low population, only 26 deaths)
Spain - 363
San Marino - 1,032 (low population, only 35 deaths)
Source: Worldometer - 12.05 12/4/20

I add the following:

USA - 62 - despite the high number of deaths you hear in the news, the deaths per 1M population are still relatively low. Mainstream media seem keen to give the most pessimistic spin they can on UK figures, but I can understand why.

Thomas replies: nowhere near as negative as the UK press have been about Italy and Spain - you don't see coffins all lined up and such imagery - even though we know that funeral directors are inundated and have never been busier! <end>

I am saddened to hear the news that Tim Brooke-Taylor (of *The Goodies* fame) has died today with Covid-19.

The family outing is brief - we drop Ed off to purchase essential supplies at the local mini-market and wait until he puts them in the boot of the car. He makes the uphill walk home alone - leaving an Easter egg on a doorstep en route - to busy himself with washing the outside windows of our home. That just makes me feel worse about my comments of yesterday. I could not be any more proud of a step-son if he were my own son. I treat him as if he were my own and I am grateful that he tolerates me and my many failings.

The rest of us park up about a mile away and set off on an exercise walk. It is, sadly, much less frequent than a daily routine, but I do wish we could all be in the mood for doing it more regularly.

It is as enjoyable to be out in the fresh air on a sunny day as it is to see Beth out of the house, enjoying herself, like a child younger than her 16 years. A child free of teenage angst, gender fluidity discussions - or whatever it is she and her peers seem to discuss at all hours - and her usual internet distractions. We spend a lovely hour or so and, despite it being nowhere near either of the two Golden Hours in the day, I do manage to take plenty of usable photos - mainly landscapes and close-up details on the beach - from our happy time spent together. Beth does not grant me permission to show any of her though and, although she maybe did not intend it to, that does always sting somewhat.

The daily Coronavirus press conference a little later disappoints on many levels. The quality of the contributors suggests that many have grown tired of it.

The mince and spaghetti supper I cook for Ed and I later on is a lot more satisfying. So too is the delicious Easter egg my darling Laura bought for me - one of two I received: Beth also gave me one of her BOGOF Easter eggs - that was a lovely surprise!

As ever, I enjoy working my magic on the photos late into the night and, eventually, I post two albums - one of which is virtually straight out of the camera and one which clearly is not.

It turned out a good day in the end.

Photos on Pages 41-43 were taken in Maryport on Sunday, 12th April 2020

DAY 16

Easter Monday *(13/4/20)*

I dreamt Laura and I were viewing a house by the sea. We loved it so much we put in an offer there and then. It was an unusual house - it had two sections of wall that were just made out of glass. The sea came to half-way up the glass. We put in an offer as soon as we saw the seals and the sea lions - that was just before we saw porpoises and dolphins leaping through the water close by.

There was nothing about the rest of the day that followed that lived up to the expectations brought about by that dream.

It was a day of frustration and anger about silly, thoughtless little acts of annoyance accumulated over time - not just ones of today. That's what I thought, but it was just really me having a really bad day. It was me to blame and me that would have to apologise to everyone else later. I have to do a lot of apologising and its something I don't mind doing, whereas some others seem to think it's a sign of weakness and they would rather sulk all day, tit-for-tat style, than drop their guard.

It has been hard to find the motivation to fill these pages over the last couple of days. Even harder to find the right words to provide anything interesting or remotely meaningful to myself, let alone anyone else who may be reading this.

For all this, I do sincerely apologise. I added 'sincerely' later. I'll cover my bets and simply say that "I apologise": For all this, I do apologise.

43

DAY 17

Tuesday 14th April 2020

I went to bed early on Monday night, but couldn't sleep. A mate insisted I watch a video of a frustrated doctor in San Diego bemoaning deaths of babies being incorrectly recorded as Covid-19 deaths and advising us to increase our intake of zinc - remember that funny-tasting water? - and quinine - gin and tonic time! I get up in the early hours of Tuesday morning and exchange a few comments on an opinion piece in *The Guardian* online. It contains a mention of the non-reporting of 'deaths per 1 M population' - a favourite bugbear of mine.

My attention is drawn by another commenter to page 51 of the following report (see page 45) from Public Health England which I downloaded whilst having a cup of tea downstairs at 03:14. I record my private thoughts which I am not brave or crazy enough to post online:

"I am not and never have been against vaccination, but I do believe that it could be used with stealth as a highly effective way to limit overall population growth. I think it may have succeeded in doing this in 2017-18, but I do not know if this was by accident or by design. Maybe something similar is being achieved now but its reach was wider than its intended target age group?"

This was my comment to *The Guardian* article:

"Let's be clear, our rulers would not be caring so much about this virus if it only killed a small proportion of a) elderly and b) those with underlying health conditions. They care because it's highly contagious and can make them seriously ill or worse, as well as a wider population than a) plus b). We had something that wiped out significantly higher numbers of the elderly in England and Wales in 2017-18 that seemingly went unchecked and unnoticed (ref EWM / EWD's 2017-18 PHE / ONS). There were c.50,000 excess winter deaths in 2017-18 - the highest since 1975-76."

I go back to bed and eventually drift off to sleep.

The morning's TV news brought some harrowing news about official government death figures for Coronavirus not including non-hospital / 'deaths beyond hospital settings' and suggests the actual figure should be at least 10% higher. There is something about the plight of care homes which, there's no easy way to say this, suggests they appear to have been turned into breeding grounds for the virus away from the public's gaze - I am tempted to use the words 'killing zones'. This prompts me to reach out to any care workers on my Facebook friends list who simply need "someone to listen" to them. I cannot imagine how harrowing it must be for them right now in what I know can be a rewarding job but, can be at the best of times, a very demanding job - both physically and mentally. I make no apology for repeating myself if I have stated this before.

The excitement of the day comes from receiving delivery of a new printer, getting it all set up and printing out some stuff Ed needs for his homework. It is light years ahead of the one with which we had previously been persevering.

I catch up on private messages from a new 'friend' and cannot contain myself from posting the following on Facebook:

"This DOWN-GRADING happened about 4 days before the Government told us we were going into lockdown and they've since introduced a 358-page Bill that introduces lots and lots of draconian long-term measures and powers over TWO YEARS that will have far-reaching consequences on all our freedoms. Who knew?"

This was prompted by seeing the following from Gov.co.uk:

Status of COVID-19

As of 19 March 2020, COVID-19 is no longer considered to be a high consequence infectious diseases (HCID) in the UK.

The 4 nations public health HCID group made an interim recommendation in January 2020 to classify COVID-19 as an HCID. This was based on consideration of the UK HCID criteria about the virus and the disease with information available during the early stages of the outbreak. Now that more is known about COVID-19, the public health bodies in the UK have reviewed the most up to date information about COVID-19 against the UK HCID criteria. They have determined that several features have now changed; in particular, more information is available about mortality rates (low overall), and there is now greater clinical awareness and a specific and sensitive laboratory test, the availability of which continues to increase.

The Advisory Committee on Dangerous Pathogens (ACDP) is also of the opinion that COVID-19 should no longer be classified as an HCID.

The need to have a national, coordinated response remains, but this is being met by the government's COVID-19 response.
<end>

The 358-page Government Bill referred to above is the Coronavirus Act 2020. A quick online search shows that it is available for download (for any interested insomniacs there may be out there!).

I may regret it later and I do concede that some sort of lockdown measures were needed, irrespective of a downgrade, but this Government has been getting far too easy a ride throughout all of this. I deleted it after 57 minutes. I rarely just leave stuff up on Facebook indefinitely these days.

I am also recommended to read the political postings of Vernon Coleman. At first glance he does not seem to be on the same political wavelength as myself, but I do quickly find some common ground. A lot of common ground, it has to be said, and I while away an hour or so whilst keeping an eye on my PMs or 'Care-worker Hotline'!

No-one messages me. I was slightly more popular before this all began, but not by much.

The economy forecast figures add further depression to that brought about by the earlier news of the day. 10% unemployment levels will be a realistic possibility and we could see the biggest shrinking of the economy (and hit to GDP) in any of our lifetimes - worse even than any of the World Wars!

I interrupt the doom and gloom to say we all had baked potatoes for tea. It was a rare and splendid moment of unity! I will ignore the fact that we had various differing individual accompaniments and focus on the togetherness that only a baked potato can bring.

I cannot remember the last time the starring role on a plate was the same for each of us. I should have taken a photograph but, sadly, one ate alone and another one ate after the other two. Oh well, you cant have everything!

I am encouraged by Channel 4 News reporting that 80% of people have died from
something other than...

'something related to Coronavirus'.

The latest deaths per 1M population are arguably not as bad as one may have been expecting and show that the UK has now overtaken The Netherlands (and Belgium has overtaken Italy).

Coronavirus deaths per 1 Million population:
World - 16 (for reference); Switzerland - 136; Netherlands - 172; UK - 178;
France - 241; Italy - 348; Belgium - 359;
Andorra - 375 (low population, only 29 deaths); Spain - 386;
San Marino - 1,061 (low population, only 36 deaths)
(countries with less than 10 deaths are excluded by me)
Source: Worldometer - 19.20 14/4/20

(Here I have ranked from 9th worst to worst country. Later on I will be much more inclined to rank from worst to, for example, 10th worst.)
But let us not dwell on these figures and just remember instead that baked potato moment and rejoice in it!

'A Celebration Of Baked Potato'
Ink Drawing - 2022

DAY 18

Wednesday 15th April 2020

News came through late last night of the death from Covid-19 of a former rugby team-mate of mine, Mike Rogerson, aged 63. I was very saddened to hear this. We played in the same amateur rugby league team over 30 years ago. Our paths would cross occasionally over the years - often whilst he would be working in a gang on the roads as I was walking by. He would always stop to shout hello or chat and always seemed to be happy and smiling. He was the first person I knew personally to die with the virus. I come across a relative of Mike's online and I put a post on the Dalston ARL Facebook page informing team-mates who may not have heard the sad news. It also appeals on behalf of the relative for photos and memories for a tribute video she is wanting to make.

BBC News informs us that a 99-year old former Army Captain, Tom Moore, has now raised over 6 million pounds - smashing his original £1,000 target - for his NHS Charities Together fundraising campaign. Tom will be 100 later this month and is doing 100 lengths of his 25-metre garden, using his walking-frame for support, to help raise funds. Tom had hip surgery in 2018 following a break and has also had NHS treatment for skin cancer to his head. Whatever the final amount (and it had increased to £8M by 18.30) eventually turns out to be, it's a wonderful achievement!

Elsewhere, we get equally wonderful news that a 106-year old great-grandmother from Birmingham is believed to be the UK's oldest patient to leave hospital after treatment for Coronavirus. May she live long and prosper! Oh, wait a minute...!

It is 31 years today since the Hillsborough disaster where 96 Liverpool fans sadly lost their lives. You may recall seeing a black and white photograph of a young Liverpool fan sat on the wall, pitch-side of the Leppings Lane terrace with his head in his hands, his Liverpool scarf held up to his eyes. That young fan was Dave Roland. He died, aged 65, at the Royal Liverpool Hospital on 6th April 2020 after suffering from Covid-19. He was pictured after trying to save the life of victim Henry Rogers in 1989. Mr. Roland's daughter said: "We have received so many messages from people who have explained the impact Dad had on their lives, from taking so many to their first Liverpool game standing them on a box in the Kop, to pouring out words of advice which some men are now saying changed their lives, even keeping them out of prison."

The girls and I had a 'girlie afternoon' watching *The Grinch* (cartoon movie version) on the sofa together. It was Beth's choice of movie and no-one cared one jot about it being 'seasonally inappropriate'. Ed joined us for pizza and mozzarella sticks with dips for tea as we watched the latest Coronavirus press conference. If Matt Hancock answered half of the many questions put to him - questions mainly exposing the government's many failings along this Coronavirus journey - then I must have missed the majority of them. Transparency seemed as rare as The Grinch's generosity towards the people of Whoville, although Hancock did serve up a good helping of waffle!

Photos taken in Maryport on 17/4/20 (except bottom right - 12/4/20).

DAY 19

New mattress day! *(16/4/20)*

Yes, today the new super-king-size mattress we ordered got delivered. It's ridiculously expensive in my opinion, but there was 41% off and I *do* love a bargain! It has a 200-day 'money-back' guarantee. 200 days is a long time. At the moment it feels like a *very* long time - very much could change within the next 200 days. If I'm still here in 200 days' time I may re-visit, nay - *will* revisit - this page and detail exactly what changed and when. I'm sure you're really looking forward to it.

Imagine if you're reading this 200 days or more after today, Thursday 16th April 2020, and there is no 200-day update? You'll be thinking I must have snuffed it or I maybe just couldn't be arsed or maybe that I forgot or maybe that nothing *did* actually change. Please think that I've left this mortal coil for a better place, then just be relieved or disappointed or really pissed off to discover me being alive. Forget that it may be because I couldn't really be arsed to work out what day the day 200 days from now really is.

Of course we may or may not be returning the mattress within 200 days or you could be reading this on day 50 and we may still be satisfied with it and maybe won't return it until day 77 or day 143 or whatever. I suspect we will not be returning it at all if it has to go back in its original packaging!

<This space is to be used for the 200-day update>

OK - I'd say don't buy the mattress with the 4-letter girl's name beginning with 'E'. Because I'm a lot heavier than my wife it's way more squashed on my side of the bed and it's quite a steep slope to climb if it's Xmas or my birthday and I'm fancying a fumble! If she was nearing moderately incontinent I'd definitely be sleeping in the deep end and the only positive is the floor is closer if I happen to roll down the slope and fall out of bed!

We get a card through the door from Maryport Community Emergency Response. I think it's absolutely wonderful that volunteers like Pam and Paul from 'Elbra' are offering to pick up shopping or urgent supplies, post mail or simply offer a friendly phone call to those who are self-isolating. They are an example of thousands of people doing similar valuable work across the countries of the UK.

At 5 p.m. Dominic Raab, the Foreign Secretary, announces that the current lockdown must be extended for at least the next 3 weeks. The BBC summarise / paraphrase Raab's comments by saying that now is not the moment to give the virus a second chance and 'your efforts are paying off'. The announcement receives mixed reviews in our household. I think it's sensible to extend the lockdown and it was expected to increase by at least a further two weeks.

We keep hearing now about something called 'R' during these press conferences. Keeping 'R' below '1' seems to be a good thing. All three spokespersons mention the 'R' in relation to graphs. I don't know when this first started to happen - it seems to very recent thing, but I don't ever recall anyone introducing us to 'R' and explaining what the 'R' actually is, i.e. what it means or what is stands for. It must mean Rate (or Ratio perhaps?).

BBC News continues with an update to Captain Tom's fund-raising total. It now exceeds FIFTEEN MILLION POUNDS! and he has completed his target of 100 legs of his walk across his garden.

I feel totally inadequate. I only managed to raise a mere £90 or so towards my target for the Great North Air Ambulance Service and I only managed to solicit poems from Laura for my proposed compilation: 'Poems of Hope - Overcoming Adversity.' I don't let it get me down, however, as it was funding that GNAA would not have otherwise received and I can spare the £50 '1st Prize Winner' (nominated charity!) donation I made to them this morning.

My best mate (who supports GNAA anyway) said he would give them a bit extra - any donation he makes will be the "or so" after the £90. He reckons that people would be reluctant to contribute via Facebook and that I should have done it through 'Just Giving'. Oh well, you live and learn! I decided to put up a copy of the receipt for the £50 but made no further comments about the poetry competition on Facebook.

Laura was mildly peeved that I didn't let her win the competition and chose to give it to GNAA instead of an animal charity, but I think that Dominic Raab is now the one with whom she has the biggest beef!

....

Mr. & Mrs. Chimney-Pot Watching The Sunset Together!

DAY 20

Friday 17th April 2020

In a live Commons Health Committee video conference live on BBC, Matt Hancock reveals that 'R' is the rate of transmission. He mentions this as part of his answer to a question from Jeremy Hunt after Mr. Hunt reminds him of the WHO conditions regarding 'tracking and tracing' of Coronavirus that need to be met before a lockdown can be lifted.

The following are the latest deaths per 1 Million population from Worldometer:

World - 18.9
China - 3 (I mention this only because it has been revised upwards by 50% - from 2!)
Ireland - 98
USA - 105
Channel Islands - 109
Luxembourg - 110
Sweden - 132
Switzerland - 149
Netherlands - 193
UK - 202
France - 275
Italy - 367
Spain - 413
Andorra - 427 (low population, only 33 deaths)
Belgium - 445
San Marino - 1,120 (low population, only 38 deaths)
Source: Worldometer - 11.07 17/4/20
(countries with less than 10 deaths are excluded)

We keep hearing about the importance of testing, we are being told that there is currently spare capacity for testing that is not being utilised, but we continue to be testing at a rate that is a fraction of the levels at which we are required to be.

I cannot remember if I posted this or not:

Very mystifying that we have spare capacity yet we are way below where we should be in testing for Coronavirus. It was interesting listening to the live Commons Health Committee video conference this morning to discover that the WHO guidelines on testing and tracking/tracing would never have permitted us to leave lockdown because we are nowhere near meeting our obligations. I'm not a fan, but I speak as I find, and I give credit where it's due and I was very impressed with Jeremy Hunt and not so much with Matt Hancock throughout. I guess that just demonstrates how low the bar has dropped with this government.

Matt Hancock: "Each month about 10,000 people die in care homes." That's before Coronavirus came along. It could now be 11-20,000.

Laura, Beth and I had a great walk along the prom and I took some photos during it and also some of the lovely sunset later. I particularly liked a photo of two chimney-pots in sharp focus: Mr & Mrs Chimney Pot Watching The Sunset Together! (Page 51)

Photos on Pages 53-54 taken in Maryport on Friday, 17th April 2020

DAY 21

Saturday 18th April 2020

Laura and I watched a Netflix movie called *Whatever Happened To Monday?*

It was about a group of septuplets who had managed to grow up as the same 'only child' whilst avoiding escape from detection, in a time decades into the future where over-population had resulted in families not being allowed to have more than one child. Children were reputed to be getting suspended in a cryogenic state until such times as populations were low enough for them to be brought back to life. It turned out later that they were actually being put to sleep and disposed of. I am acutely aware of futuristic twaddle from 10 or 20 years ago now being an accepted part of everyday life, so it's not so easy nowadays to dismiss very much as 'too far-fetched'.

I gave Ed a lift to B & M to hand in a copy of his C.V. - they're looking for staff and he's after a job to keep him occupied until he returns to 6th Form at Netherhall School. It was a non-essential journey and probably contravenes lock-down regulations. I've never seen the car park so busy. I wait in the car and Ed joins the back of quite a long queue - it's one in, one out. After about 20 minutes with Ed now near the front of the queue, his mate's mother (who works there) makes an appearance and kindly takes in the C.V. for him with outstretched arm. Ed never made it into the shop to purchase anything - that would have added risk, but could have legitimised our travel. Days have become filled with such minor internal conflicts or, hitherto, trivial dilemmas and people sometimes take to social media now to solicit permission before undertaking such journeys.

I watched a video to listen to some poems from Speakeasy at Foxes in Carlisle from 2015 that had been put onto their Facebook page. The standard of work was very high. There were a few people I recognised and some people I'd never met - that included some that had participated in the recent 'Speakeasy Meets Poetry Out Loud' video conference - and others that I had heard of, including the late Nick Pemberton. I was sorry I never got the opportunity to meet him. I admired the enthusiasm shown by him and everyone present and decided that I maybe should try and put a bit more effort into any future poetry 'performances' that I attempt to make.

A little before 3 p.m. I tune into BBC Radio Cumbria to listen to a recording of Liverpool v Carlisle United F.C. - a 1-1 drawn game after 90 minutes and still 1-1 after extra-time that we (Carlisle) lost 3-2 on a penalty shoot-out. It was an EFL 'League' Cup 3rd Round match that Ed and I attended at Anfield on Wednesday 23rd September 2015. There was a great atmosphere on the night and the recording does the memory justice. The Carlisle fans are making a lot of noise. Carlisle go behind, but I cheer Derek Asamoah's equaliser for Carlisle just as much as if it were a live game on the radio and there's a tear in my eye. You probably would need to have experienced the good and bad times of being a football fan for a few years to begin to understand how football can move one so - either that or a sentimental old sod like me!

It doesn't seem like four and a half years ago since we were chanting 'U-ni-ted, u-ni-ted!' on the night Carlisle took Liverpool very close. There were 42,518 fans at Anfield and the radio commentator is disappointed that he has not been made aware of the away attendance (of c.6,000). We got a very different half-time interval experience - this time it is interrupted with the latest Coronavirus announcement.

I think of absent friends - my pal Adrian Scott who died suddenly in 2019, aged 53. Adrian, a long-standing C Stand season-ticket holder at Brunton Park, was one of a small group of us who used to travel to most away games together for a good few seasons. He once painted his Ford Orion in Carlisle United's memorable 'deckchair' away shirt strip colours and made the local weekly free paper stood on top of it. I open up a bottle of *Crabbie's Alcoholic Ginger Beer* and toast Adrian's memory!

The original photo of my late friend Adrian Scott featured in the (now defunct) *Cumbrian Gazette*. Photographer unknown.

DAY 22

Sunday 19th April 2020

I post these latest 'stats' every couple of days. They are markers in the sands of time. They plot progress along a dangerous journey. I hope they help people in some small way. They are a way to help people keep a truer perspective than the one that I feel the media are sometimes trying to impose on us with their tendency to give the most pessimistic outlook.

Coronavirus deaths per 1 Million population:
World - 20.7
Luxembourg - 115 (low population, only 72 deaths)
Ireland - 116
USA - 118
Channel Islands - 121 (low population, only 21 deaths)
Sweden - 150
Switzerland - 158
Netherlands - 210
UK - 228
France - 296
Italy - 384
Spain - 437
Andorra - 453 (low population, only 35 deaths)
Belgium - 490
San Marino - 1,149 (low population, only 39 deaths)
Source: Worldometer - 12.30 19/4/20
(excludes countries with less than 10 deaths and countries with less than 100 deaths per 1M)

Beth gets annoyed with me for asking her questions about shortbread, when she makes a rare appearance to eat a brunch that her mum has made for her, and I get annoyed with her and tell her to go to her room. I go up a few minutes later to apologise and get annoyed with her "go away...!" after the third time she says it. I storm off, saying something like "you would love it if I went away for good" and I regret it immediately, but I cannot apologise straight away without making the situation worse.

I take advantage of Laura being busy with some work outside and watch one of my recent purchases - a double DVD of Marillion live at the Royal Abert Hall. I have never been a *massive* fan of Marillion, but I must say the music and the performance is stunning - absolutely superb.

Ed got dressed up in a white short-sleeved shirt, a black, floral-print tie and smart shorts to host a quiz for himself and his mates on Zoom. His mum bought him a big bottle of beer to enjoy specially for the occasion. We do not see him again for the rest of the night.

Laura and I spend the evening playing Scrabble. It starts off very light-hearted. It is a close encounter. Towards the end of the game, when there are very few tiles remaining in the bag we both get very competitive. The scores are level - desperate measures are called upon - and we manage to finish the game with a decisive winner. Accusations of cheating had come and gone, but we both admit how enjoyable it had been and we start to watch the first half of a movie together, before bedtime.

Just before bedtime Beth tells me she has forgiven me for earlier and I do the same. We both exchange 'love yous' and all is well in our world.

DAY 23

Monday 20th April 2020

I am sleeping better on the new mattress - I didn't get up once to pee last night! "Did you pee the bed?" the 'Black Dog' which accompanied my snoozing enquires. "No!" I say sharply as I jump out of bed and he toddles off indignantly.

I dreamt well too. I had been receiving one-to-one personal tuition from a moderatively attractive lady less than half my age. It had been a work training-course and our pairing had finished slightly later than everyone else. A few of her colleagues were already having drinks in the facility's bar. "What will you do now?" I ask. She shoves a couple of drinks in my hands and says "come on" and we head to a bustling city centre with loads of people stood outside bars, drinks in hand. Everyone is wanting to fill our empty glasses with their spare drinks. We are both drinking lager and white wine and it's becoming difficult to make sure we get the right drinks poured into the right glasses. We never buy a drink. The free alcohol is flowing and it occurs to me that she is becoming more attractive with every sip. We move from bar to bar (without ever going inside) and chat to groups of different people - I remember one group being Glasgow Celtic fans, but they wore no colours.

We are having a great time socialising when, suddenly, we break off and we are alone. I realise she is wearing much less clothes than before. She looks a bit like Pocahontas, but with golden hair. Her well-toned body is bronzed and covered with lots of long horizontal scars. They are like long zips - some of which appear opened up to reveal a different texture - that of a healed wound. I don't know if this is from some tribal ritual or from years of very deliberate self-harm. She looks strangely beautiful, but she tells me that she is annoyed with me because I have not shown any sign of being outwardly attracted to her. I mumble something about that not necessarily meaning that I wasn't, then I wake up. The dream has gone. I will leave it to the analysts to figure out what, if anything, it all means!

The 'Black Dog' returns when Laura heads off alone to do some much-needed grocery shopping. It is hard for me to do anything out of doors when he's around. Some of the neighbours in the line of four terraced properties down the hill from us are out in their front garden - one couple seem to spend most of their waking life out there when the sun is shining - and we look down on them, being an end terrace higher up the hill. Three of the four properties share a common front path. I feel sorry for the couple in the middle of this block of three as we never see the woman that lives there sat out and only seem to see the man sat out when one of the neighbouring couples has gone out shopping.

I want to go outside and plant up some violas in our tubs, but the presence of the 'ever-presents' deters shy old me - more-so today because Laura has informed me that the woman is enjoying the sunshine and has her top lifted up and her bra on show. It will be a brave gardener that ventures forth today!

DAY 24

Tuesday 21st April 2020

I have been posting these figures on Facebook every other day. I rarely get any comments and just the odd like and have no idea if anyone values this information, but it feels to me like an important task to regularly update them. I will be posting the next update three days from now.

Coronavirus deaths per 1 Million population:
World - 22
Isle Of Man - 106 (low population, only 9 deaths)
Luxembourg - 120 (low population, only 75 deaths)
USA - 128
Channel Islands - 138 (low population, only 24 deaths)
Ireland - 139
Sweden - 156
Switzerland - 166
Netherlands - 229
Sint Maarten - 233 (low population, only 10 deaths)
UK - 243
France - 310
Italy - 399
Spain - 455
Andorra - 479 (low population, only 37 deaths)
Belgium - 518
San Marino - 1,179 (low population, only 40 deaths)
Source: Worldometer - 13.15 21/4/20
(excludes countries with less than 100 deaths per 1M)

The BBC continues to give the most pessimistic news about death figures. There is a heart-breaking story of a disabled lady dying in care - they show footage of her playing the drums. The sudden rise in reported deaths in care figures is alarming.

The news also mentions a slump in oil prices - temporarily dropping to below zero! We may see fuel prices drop to below £1 a litre if we are lucky!

I manage to get out for a bit and plant up some of our tubs with the pansies and violas that Laura bought a couple of weeks ago. I hope to try and do something with the front garden in the next few days (and weeks!).

I got two deliveries today: two Tangerine Dream CDs and a cheap (discontinued-ish!) XXL T-shirt from their online store Eastgate in Germany and some Wharfedale speakers to allow me to listen to CDs better - i.e. when I am *not* listening through wired headphones in bed.

The BBC annoys me by saying the UK has its highest death toll for 20 years without giving the important statistics behind it or further details explaining the timescale behind it. I find this on the ITV website:

"England and Wales recorded its highest weekly death toll for 20 years, largely due to the number of coronavirus deaths, figures from the Office for National Statistics show. The figures, which take into account deaths outside of hospitals, recorded the provisional number of deaths registered in England and Wales as 18,516 in the week of April 10. This is an increase of 2,129 deaths compared to the previous week and 7,996 deaths more than the five-year average. It is also the largest amount of deaths in the UK since the first week of 2000"

One third of the *weekly* "highest deaths for 20 years" figures mention Coronavirus on the death certificate. I post the following on facebook:

Ok, we have the highest WEEKLY death total for 20 years - that's during the peak of the worst pandemic we've had in our lifetimes.

In 2017-18 excess winter deaths were the highest since 1975-76 - that was the highest for FORTY-TWO YEARS - possibly even the highest after Coronavirus! Who knows? We'll hopefully find out in November when the 2019-20 figures are published.

Those c.50,000 deaths (in England and Wales only) in 2017-18 were over a season of several months. Why has that been ignored and omitted from comparison graphs? Why didn't we hear a peep from anyone then or afterwards? What happened then that has seemingly been covered up by government?

Reeni: What's your point caller? Folk not dying enough to make the top league! Some fitba fans taken it too far

ME: Hi Reeni, hope you are all well! I care about people dying. I care as much about all the people who died in 2017-18 as all the people who are dying now. Plenty of other people are caring about the ones who have died now, rightly so, but not so much for the ones who died two years ago who we didn't know about at the time it would seem. I am raising awareness for these people who appear to have no-one speaking for them. I am highlighting something that I think is important, possibly linked to this pandemic. That, and giving a bit of perspective.

Reeni: guid points well made thanks <end>

There is a red sky tonight. Venus glistens above the horizon. I decide to go out and take some photos of it using the camera on my phone. Later, I go to the trouble of setting up my tripod and attaching the longest lens I have on my Nikon D7500. The lens gives the equivalent of a 900mm lens at its longest. It proves to be difficult to get a long-exposure image free from camera-shake, but I manage to get a few photos I can put up on Facebook.

A friend asks me if I saw the satellites. A penny drops. I had seen what I thought were aircraft moving across the sky, in the distance, when I had my phone outside earlier, but I failed to photograph them. The same friend alerts me to the scheduled reappearance of the satellites at 4.04 a.m.

A list of things that I think might have had some bearing on the effectiveness of the 2019-20 flu vaccine:

A change from egg-based to cell-based flu vaccine production; 'Aussie Summer Flu' having more significance on proceedings than usual; a global delay in the circulation of the flu vaccine; more strains than usual needing to be added to the flu vaccine formula; lots of anecdotal reports of people experiencing symptoms very similar to those of Covid-19 in late 2019 and January and February 2020; Covid-19.

Other stuff that may be of interest:

I thought that I had discovered that 40% of the World's flu vaccines were produced in China, but I can no longer find any info to support that claim; the political situation between China and Trump's USA has been less than favourable - hence a conspiracy theory circulating re: Covid-19 is a form of bio-warfare; Covid-19 reputedly broke out in China immediately after some vaccine testing.

Some interesting flu vaccination statistics:

It was reported on 13th February 2020 that a record 81% of North Cumbria NHS Trust hospital staff had had the flu vaccine. Approximately 75% of over-65s in the UK receive the flu vaccine each year.

I discussed all of the above in 2020, but only added it here in 2022.

Brave Old Sequence (extract)

Mid seventies, late in the evening
Under the covers of my single bed
Red ball on a chrome chain radio
Mono speaker to my head
New exciting sounds
Nowhere else could be found
My dreams were always Tangerine, heard
On the airwaves of Radio Luxembourg

DAY 25

Wednesday 22nd April 2020

I was up before 4 a.m. I went out with my camera and a wide-ranging zoom lens. I might have seen a couple of satellites (with flashing lights?) in the far distance, but they did not make for a photo opportunity. I took a few hand-held long exposures but they showed no light streaks that would suggest fast-moving objects nearby. I had managed to trip over objects on the ground on both my trip round to the front of my house and on the way back again. The resulting noise seemed much amplified in the early hours of the morning and I worried about being mistaken for an intruder! I treat the bewildered cats to an extra, early breakfast of cat biscuits - they will get meat or fish later - make myself tea and biscuits and wash half of the washing-up pile left from yesterday. Then I go back to bed.

After a late breakfast, I enjoy watching the first ever *virtual* Prime Minister's Questions. Dominic Raab deputises for Boris Johnson and Matt Hancock answers questions also. It seems to be an exercise in blame deflection. We appear to have been slow on everything, but it is always someone else to blame and there is no admission of failings, but a healthy dose of lies accompanies the government responses. The first comes early on when Raab accuses Keir Starmer, the new labour leader, of being mistaken - merely to deflect from the government's failing to achieve more than 18,000 tests in a day when the target to be achieved in 8 days' time is 100,000 a day - and mentions that there is capacity to test 40,000 people a day. Raab knows full well the discussion was about actual tests being carried out and not capacity to test. Starmer, thankfully, does not tolerate this and soon puts Raab in his place.

The day ends up being one of disappointment - disappointment in myself. I don't do work on the front garden. I don't participate in an Earth Day online poetry event where I could have read out the poem that I had recently published. Not even Ed's delicious home-made bread made with spelt flour lifts my spirits. I am out of sorts for no good reason.

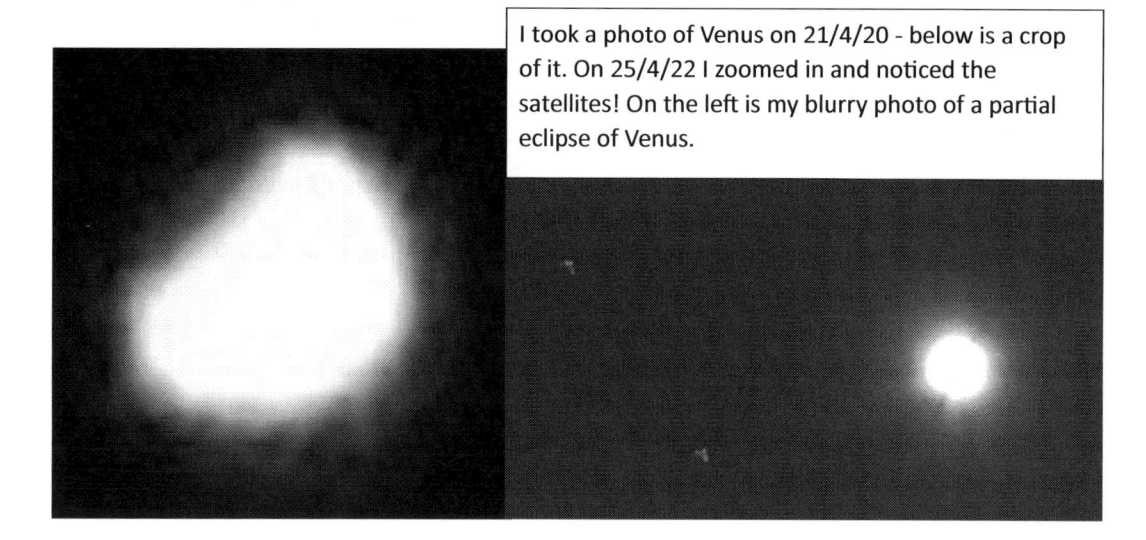

I took a photo of Venus on 21/4/20 - below is a crop of it. On 25/4/22 I zoomed in and noticed the satellites! On the left is my blurry photo of a partial eclipse of Venus.

DAY 26

Thursday 23rd April 2020

St. George's Day apparently.

The Feast of Saint George.

Dragon-slaying clap-trap has never interested me less than today.

Today is…

A blank day

I have…

A blank mind

A blank life

A blank page*

Can you spot the birdie in this crappy sunset photo, taken on this day?

*Blank aside from this shite!

OK, it's not a blank page, I do realise that - it's just a bit sparse! And a bit of naffness that I've just made naffer in 2022!

DAY 27

Friday 24th April 2020

I had a bad dream last night. I had a girlfriend who looked attractive until she removed her teeth. I was unaware that some of her teeth were not her own. I did not have the heart to finish with her and so I kept on with the relationship. That probably makes my *dream* me, at least, appear shallow - or perhaps it is the reverse! I think my dream is an allegory for continuing to struggle on (mentally) through the lockdown - however toothless (!) it is making me feel right now - and how incredibly impotent I feel to be able do anything to make a difference or to change my pessimistic view of what the future may hold for us all.

I have come across a lot of video footage suggesting similarities between parts of the 2012 Olympics opening ceremony created by Danny Boyle and the coronavirus pandemic. At face value parts of it do seem to be very prophetic but, on balance, I think this is purely coincidental.

I continue to get annoyed by some of the footage I see featuring NHS staff. Now I know there are times when it will be impossible to socially-distance in hospitals, so it makes it all the more mind-boggling when you continually see no social-distancing in hospitals at all. You'd be forgiven for thinking all NHS staff got infected (or given immunity?) when c.80% of them had the flu vaccine! Rant over!

Donald Trump creates alarm world-wide (for a change) by suggesting injecting disinfectant could kill the virus. His suggestion that sufferers may benefit from a huge blast of UV light naturally pales into insignificance alongside something more nonsensical.

Today we have the Transport Secretary, Grant Shapps, giving the Government's Coronavirus Briefing. This makes sense given that what follows is mainly related to new transport measures. Some trilateral agreement with France and Ireland has been reached to ensure the smooth movement of freight. This is followed by some transport-related graphs and some medical gobbledigook.

We received a delivery of bedding plants and compost today that Laura had ordered, so I spent an hour or so planting up more tubs with Lobelia, French Marigolds, Pansies and Petunias.

We hear that retail sales were down 5% in March - I'm surprised it's not a lot worse, but it's being painted as something of a disaster and is something of a record.

Whilst trawling through the Worldometer Coronavirus statistics, I discover that Vatican City has the 2nd highest cases per 1 Million population. San Marino has the most cases per 1M.

Finally, as promised:

Coronavirus deaths per 1 Million population:
World - 24.8; Luxembourg - 133 (low population, only 83 deaths); USA - 154; Ireland - 161; Channel Islands - 167 (low population, only 29 deaths); Switzerland - 182; Isle Of Man - 188 (low population, only 16 deaths); Sweden - 213; Netherlands - 250; Sint Maarten - 280 (low population, only 12 deaths); UK - 287; France - 335; Italy - 423; Andorra - 479 (low population, only 37 deaths); Spain - 482; Belgium - 576; San Marino - 1,179 (low population, only 40 deaths).
Source: Worldometer - 16.57 24/4/20
(excludes countries with less than 100 deaths per 1M population)

Mackerel sky and sliver moon - photos taken in Maryport on 24th April 2020

TOWARDS MOCKERKIN (extract)

A clutch of bent oaks clings steadfastly atop a lonely Lakeland fell.
Time, their seasoned master - not just gnarly stubbornness.
Yearning for embraces from inquisitive kids,
Two at a time, trying and failing to touch fingertips
Around their vast, comforting trunks.
Eager to share their catkins and fill tiny acorn cups
With stories of innocence and secret melancholy.
Trees scarred by meteorological sorcery and hastily-etched love.

DAY 28

Saturday 25th April 2020

I asked Beth to cut off all my hair last night and she kindly obliged. I bent over the bath and she used her scissors. She had lots of fun doing it and it was nice to spend some time together. Laura was not amused by the end result. This morning I will need to shave myself bald to tidy up last night's work. I use scissors at first, then the same razor I use to trim around my beard.

Laura hates my lack of hair and is being absolutely horrible to me. She is saying I have only done it because I know she would hate it. She is taking photos of my head and sending them to her other daughter - mocking me. She has fallen out with me and has now gone off upstairs in a big strop. She comes down later and her mood doesn't improve, so I spend most of the rest of the day lying on the bed in our bedroom. This is in stark contrast to how Laura expects me to be whenever she has anything done to her hair. She goes in a sulk if I don't say how lovely it is - whatever I think it may look like. In defence, she asks how I would react if she shaved her head. I tell her that I would love her just as much and she can do whatever she wants to her hair.

Anyway, enough of that. I find out today that San Marino - the country with most coronavirus deaths per 1 Million population by miles - was the test country and the first in Europe to install 5G. Now that isn't quite the same as saying 5G causes Coronavirus, but - **bloody hell!** - what a truly extraordinary coincidence. Surprisingly, I have found nothing to suggest that this information was that which sparked any of the much-publicised 5G Coronavirus conspiracies - so I can only draw the conclusion that it wasn't. Maybe I'm the only person in the World who has noticed this bizarre statistic! I must admit that I never knew anything about San Marino before this all started. I knew it existed, but that was it. It appears that two types of 5G testing were carried out in San Marino. I also learn that the country is totally land-locked by Italy, its population is a little over 33,000 and lots of them have been tested for the virus - 40, sadly, having died with it to date. San Marino has about twice as many deaths per 1M population as any other country in the world and about four times as many (per 1M) as the UK has currently.

DAY 29

Sunday 26th April 2020

The stalemate between Laura and I continues - my fault, I ignored her when she asked if I wanted a cup of tea.

Ed has been watching *After Life* Season 2 by Ricky Gervais on Netflix. He, Laura and I loved Season 1. I watch the final one and a half episodes of it with him whilst having my brunch. Laura took off upstairs when I came down - that's why I ignored her later. Its petty, but there are far worse things to worry about right now - not least Boris Johnson's return to work tomorrow!

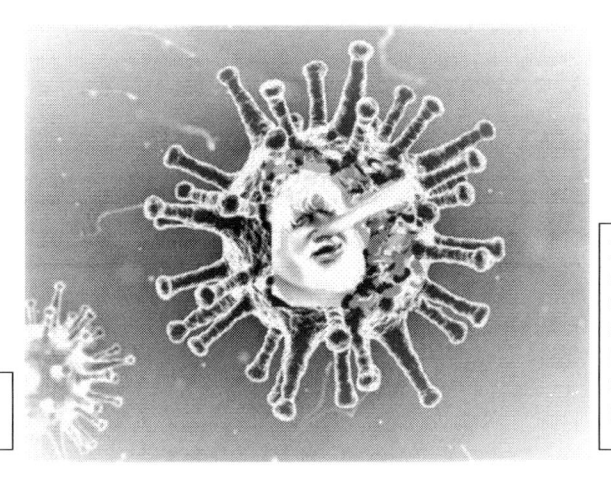

'Coronaboris'
2022

I crudely created this using a modified photograph of a strain of Japanese 'B' flu and a modified caricature of Boris with a 'Pinocchio' nose. The original artist and photographer are unknown.

I look for some more short poems which may seem relevant enough to pepper the blank bits of space there may otherwise be in parts of this diary, in-between watching the shockingly cheeky vulgarity and the poignant sadness contained within Gervais's brilliant tragi-comedy.

Ed disappears upstairs when it finishes and I eventually make another drink to take outside and catch some fresh air. I sit across a silent table from Laura, drinking my tea and dunking some rich tea biscuits. I get up and fill a watering-can to water the newly-planted tubs - the sky clouded over a couple of hours or more ago and there is no risk of scorching the plants. I refill the can a couple of times more and sit down again, but still there is silence.

I go inside and put on a music DVD - a live concert of Tangerine Dream playing solo compositions of their late leader, Edgar Froese. It was recorded long before his death. I watch it from roughly where I think I stopped it the first time I played it. I had listened to miles more last time than I thought I had, but I do not click forward. I have plenty of time these days.

At 9 p.m. Laura asks me if I would like a cup of coffee and I say "yes please!".
We start conversing again.

DAY 30

Monday 27th April 2020

Boris is back!

He makes a speech of over 8 minutes letting us know how important it is to carry on keeping to the lockdown, that we are winning against the virus and thanking us for our continued compliance.

There were a few other bits and pieces along the way, but they were the main points he kept reiterating. He didn't make any gaffes, so maybe the rest has done him good.

I update my figures:

Coronavirus deaths per 1 Million population:
World - 26.6; Luxembourg - 141 (low population, only 88 deaths);
USA - 167; Switzerland - 189;
Channel Islands - 201 (low population, only 35 deaths);
Isle Of Man - 212 (low population, only 18 deaths);
Sweden - 217;
Ireland - 220;
Netherlands - 261;
Sint Maarten - 303 (low population, only 13 deaths);
UK - 305;
France - 350;
Italy - 441;
Spain - 503;
Andorra - 518 (low population, only 40 deaths);
Belgium - 622; San Marino - 1,208 (low population, only 41 deaths).

Source: Worldometer - 12.35 27/4/20
(excludes countries with less than 10 deaths and/or less than 100 deaths per 1M population)

I get up late. I have been getting up later and later of late. Phew, that is a lot of lates! No matter! It is not that long since I said I never struggle to find anything to fill my days. That is still true, to an extent, but there is little to break the routine these days, the house feels a tad less hospitable and I know I am not as happy as I could be.

I am not doing as many productive things as I would like to do - the front garden still awaits my long overdue attention. I feel guilty that I am spending longer in bed and that I am being less productive and that does not help with lifting my mood, my spirits. The days pass quickly enough without failing to stuff them with all sorts of things that semi-retirement is supposed to allow you to.

This pandemic-imposed retirement must be like being in a... retirement home?...no, not really...a prison?...no, not quite...a monastery maybe? Well, a lot of monks *do* have shaved heads, I have been very quiet and I am doing a lot of contemplating lately!

Laura and I have made our peace. I apologised for shaving my head and reminding her of her ex-husband and promised to never do it again!

We went for a lovely walk together along the promenade in the sunshine. Laura made me wear a cap; she wore a long, padded coat despite the sunshine. The tide was well in, but we managed to get down on the sandstone slabs at the back of the shore once it had dropped back slightly - that helped me increase my photo opportunities.

We walked from the furthest car park to where the promenade terminates at Maryport Golf Club and back. We stopped at the local store on our return and Laura went in to get some much-needed groceries.

Laura made a delicious chicken curry dinner for us both - the kids had cooked themselves fish (from frozen) in the oven earlier - and I enjoyed a bottle of IPA beer as I edited and tweaked my photos.

Sunset brought Venus and the Moon together and I rushed to get my camera out again to capture the moment. Later, Laura and I are snuggled up together after making love - a rare union in these times of lockdown.

Photos on Pages 69-71 & 72 (Top) were taken in Maryport on Monday, 27th April 2020

DAY 31

Tuesday 28th April 2020

Laura and I *both* get up early - that is very unusual and a sign that we are both a lot happier today.

We watch a few episodes of the Netflix series *Unorthodox* together. I wonder if the Jewish Orthodox community approve of it, whilst not really caring much either way. *So why mention it?*

Later we play Trivial Pursuit with Ed - Beth refused to participate after her brother had been constantly annoying her before, during and after a shared dinner session.

71

DAY 32

Wednesday 29th April 2020

I got up late today - can't have anyone thinking I can be happy two days in a row!

News comes through that Boris's girlfriend has given birth to their child, but he will not be taking paternity leave.

Laura took a delivery in from the step whilst the Hermes driver watched on from a distance. It was the second of two Denon CD receivers I'd been buying - this time a cheap older second hand model. I am really starting to get back into my music 'big style' albeit I'm still very much 'old tech'. These receivers, however, will allow more modern technological devices to be connected to them and the latest one even has bluetooth installed, so I can connect my MP3 player on shuffle play!

I made my second trip of lockdown to the Post Office and took an exercise walk along the promenade, taking photos - two of them below - and editing them later.

DAY 33

Thursday 30th April 2020

Captain Tom Moore is 100 today and has now raised over 30 million pounds for the NHS.

The Tory Government set a target on 2nd April of 100,000 tests per day for Coronavirus by the end of April. The deadline is today. There was a big increase to 52,000 tests on Tuesday - a figure that included a lot of re-tests - but the Government has finally admitted that it is "probable" they will not achieve their target. The reality is that they should be aiming to achieve 250,000 tests per day to meet an aim identified by no less than Boris Johnson himself.

Meanwhile, conspiracy theorist Richard D Hall made the following announcement:

Today I wrote to my MP and to the chief constable of South Wales Police. Here is what I wrote. I hope others will do the same.

Hello,

I would like to report a fraud case which is affecting everyone in my community (Merthyr Tydfil).

In October, a conference which was organised by Bill Gates in New York, discussed recommendations for a future up coming corona virus pandemic. This advice was given to the UK government.

Here is a link to that conference.

https://www.centerforhealthsecurity.org/event201/

Six weeks AFTER this conference, an outbreak of COVID-19 allegedly occurred in China, and there is evidence that the outbreak may have been a deliberate act and that the COVID-19 originated from a laboratory in Wuhan, possibly with U.S. connections.

There are MANY indications that the current "pandemic" is a billion dollar financial scam/fraud, manufactured in order to sell billions of doses of vaccine.

The current lockdown measures are unnecessary, unjustifiable (see documentation) and are a criminal act of economic terrorism against the people of the United Kingdom. I would like the police force to protect the citizens of the U.K. by investigating this crime and arresting those who are helping Bill Gates run this billion dollar fraud, and arresting those who are carrying out acts of economic terrorism (ie lockdown measures). Those who are high up in the UK government (including Boris Johnson) are primarily responsible for the economic terrorism.

Please download this document for more details,

https://cvpandemicinvestigation.com/.../THE-COVID-19-Pandemic...

Or visit this website.

https://cvpandemicinvestigation.com/

And a video examining Bill Gates and his motives here,

https://www.richplanet.net/richp_genre.php...

Thank You
Richard Hall
(I included my address and phone number)

I share Richard's post on Facebook - adding that I might not agree with all of it, but I think it's important to consider other viewpoints and not just be a happy clapper.

There'll be 'happy clapping' at 8 p.m. tonight, but I think I will no longer be taking part in it - I state this not really knowing how I will react when the hour comes round.

I continue to struggle with the fairly common-place all-singing, all-dancing videos of NHS staff - failing to social-distance most of the time - that 'media' is presenting to us, with shortages of PPE and statistics that tell us that out of three people who enter hospitals with the virus, one will die with it.

At the start of this journal I likened the lockdown situation to war, but the situation that we and the vast majority of people on social media seem to be in is one of 'making the most of a bad situation' that is nothing like a bad one - and certainly not like I imagine a war-time situation to be. I do not know if that is a 'brave face' or a natural one we are wearing, but I imagine there must, surely, be homes where someone really is fighting a war. There are homes suffering the death of a loved one and tragic stories waiting to be told, but we get a romanticised view of everything on TV and social media - or at least that's the way it seems to me.

I imagine being one of those people who really is fighting a war and truly suffering during this pandemic. I would not know where I could go to scream from the rooftops how bad things are and to describe what I am feeling right now if I was in their shoes. I don't know what place would be one in which they would find comfort or be able to unburden themselves amongst people who would listen and understand. I imagine I would feel gagged and frustrated and just sick and tired of the incessant do-gooder praise and positivity at all cost mentality. I would want to scream, not quietly cry myself to sleep at night, or maybe do both? But I am not one of these people. Maybe they just quietly go about their business doing what they are told to do, saying nothing about it to anyone else and just doing their best, making sure they just get through it as best they can, doing what's best and for the best. Best, best, best, best, best - but is it good enough? Yes, despite the one in three death rate, we do appear to have flattened the curve and turned a corner where hospital death numbers are concerned and these continue to decline. The news of deaths in care homes has, however, sadly not been so positive.

....

JACK AND MARGUERITE (excerpt)

Taking the most direct route to the dining-room now,
Slowly and solemnly he puts his palm to the glass
And waits...
Then, from out of nowhere, a hand reaches out
And pats his back, ever so gently.
"Hello Jack, would you mind coming round to reception?
I'll bring you out a chair and make us a nice cuppa.
Matron wants a word" - "Huh, what's that?" - "I said Matron wants a word.
She's been trying to ring you".

MARYPORT - 29/4/20

DAY 34

Friday 1st May 2020

Pinch, punch, first of the month! White rabbits, no return!

It is the first day of a new month. It is destined to be a better month than the last one with, hopefully, some easing of the lockdown towards the middle of it.

I get up early-ish, feed the cats and wheel the heavy black bin down the stairs - it had a week off last week! I make a cup of tea and type a few lines of this before I propose to return to bed for an hour or so.

In some respects I feel my family are fraudsters. None of us have had friends or family die from the virus. Both Laura and I are furloughed on no worse than 80% of our pay, we are managing financially - helped by our cancelled Madeira holiday - and our jobs are safe for now. My pensions will have taken a massive hit, but some of the value lost may be recovered over time. The kids have adapted well to life in lockdown and we have had no major fall-outs. We are all getting by fine. I don't envisage any long-term damage to our mental health and I don't imagine there should be much to tell about all this in five, ten, fifteen or twenty years from now - if we're all fortunate enough to still be here, living on this planet. I do realise that not everyone will be as fortunate as ourselves and that I may be severely underestimating the long-term financial and mental impact of this crisis.

Maybe in fifty or a hundred years from now my writing may serve as one of many reminders - albeit a somewhat dull reminder - of ordinary, everyday life during a pandemic. This is as honest an appraisal as I can make. When I set out to record details of this Coronavirus journey thirty-three days ago, I was not sure what direction it would take. Any fears I may have had appear to have subsided somewhat. I'd like to think I'm being realistic when I say I don't think the outcome is going to be too negative a one for my household that we can't recover successfully from it. I hope I'm not sounding or being complacent. We're keeping ourselves safe and doing the right things along with the majority of the population.

I feel well in mind, body and spirit today. I do, however, get a bit of a shock - a punch? - when I see the sharp rise in the UK deaths per 1M figures since I last posted them. It seems the non-hospital deaths (now being accurately reported?) have had quite an impact and the UK has now overtaken France.

Coronavirus deaths per 1 Million population:
World - 30.1; Luxembourg - 144 (low population, only 90 deaths); USA - 193; Switzerland - 201; Channel Islands - 230 (low population, only 40 deaths); Isle Of Man - 247 (low population, only 21 deaths); Ireland - 250; Sweden - 256; Netherlands - 280; Sint Maarten - 303 (low population, only 13 deaths); France - 373; UK - 394; Italy - 463; Spain - 525; Andorra - 544 (low population, only 42 deaths); Belgium - 655; San Marino - 1,208 (low population, only 41 deaths)
Source: Worldometer - 09.05 1/5/20
(excludes countries with less than 10 deaths and/or less than 100 deaths per 1M population)

234,253 people have died from the virus world-wide. In the UK 26,771 people have died with Covid-19. That is the 3rd highest figure - behind USA at 63,871 and Italy at 27,967.

I post this to Facebook:
UK has the 3rd highest number of deaths with Covid-19 behind USA and Italy.
UK has overtaken France in 'deaths per 1M population'. It is now the 4th worst affected country with a large population. <end>

I also add the Worldometer stats on the previous page.

I didn't bother going back to bed.

At the Government's daily press conference we hear that the target of 100,000 tests a day has finally - and somewhat miraculously - been reached and that there had been over 122,000 tests yesterday. We soon find out that that figure includes over 27,000 home testing kits and 12,000 kits destined for care homes etc. that have just been sent out this week!

Out of the blue I receive a text message from my employer. It says "URGENT Response Required. Please see…(censored)…portal for a potential new job immediate start and chance to use ~~data collection expertise~~ to help the country."

super-hero super-powers!

Well I certainly wasn't expecting that!

Photos on Pages 78-80 were taken on Saturday, 2nd May 2020, in Maryport.

DAY 35

Saturday 2nd May 2020

I am still mulling over last night's communication from my employer. I need to decide before 9 a.m. on Monday morning whether or not I wish to work during lockdown. I was hoping it was going to be a home-based opportunity, but it will involve calling on households by appointment and, from what I can gather, the collection of swabs.

Laura and I enjoy a lovely walk with Beth along the river by the harbour. I take lots of photos - as usual - and the girls stop for shopping on the way back. Later I cook supper for Ed and I - a spicy satay-style chicken curry. I cooked it from scratch using a diverse range of ingredients, including peanut butter and honey. I did some oven chips too - as per Ed's request. We both enjoyed it very much.

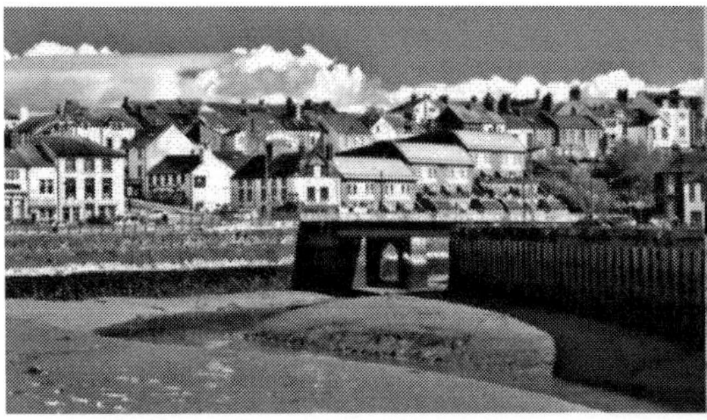
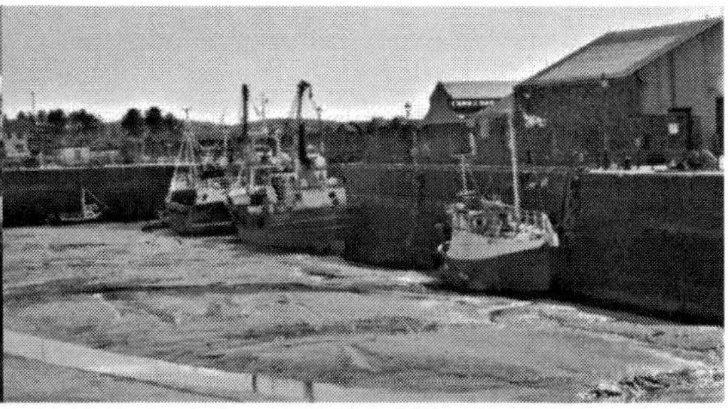
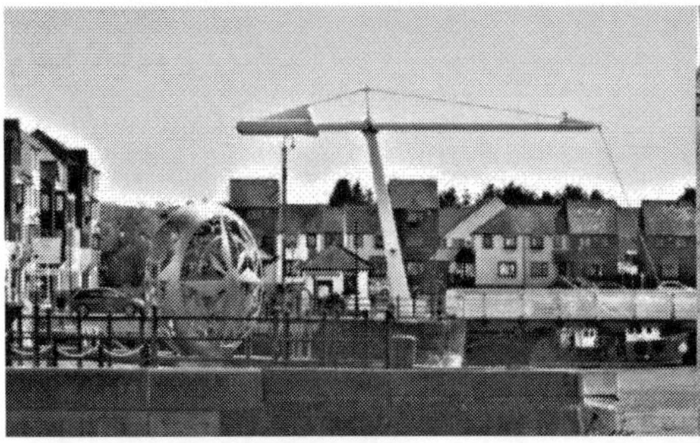
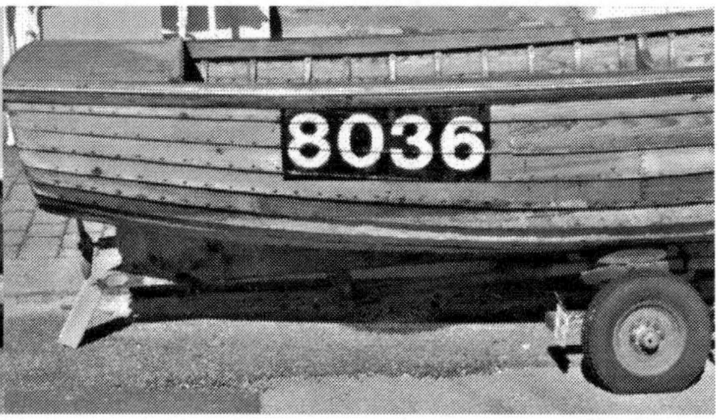
8036
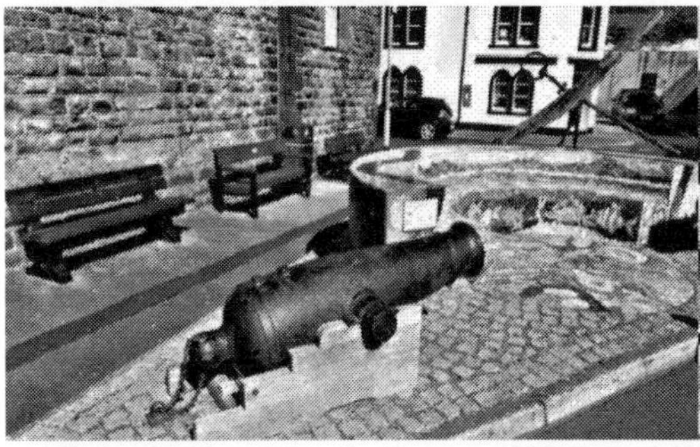
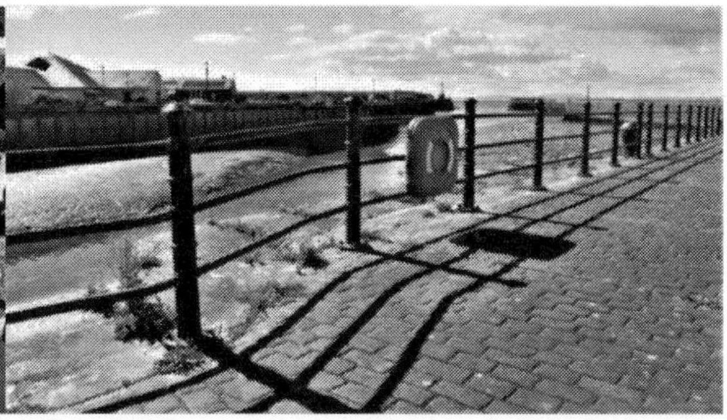
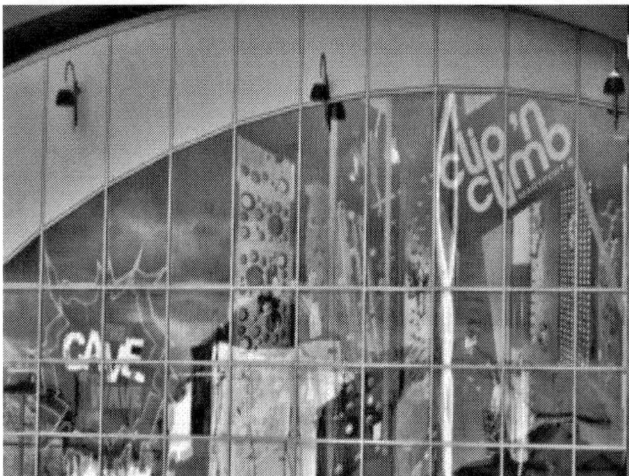
clip'n climb
CAVE
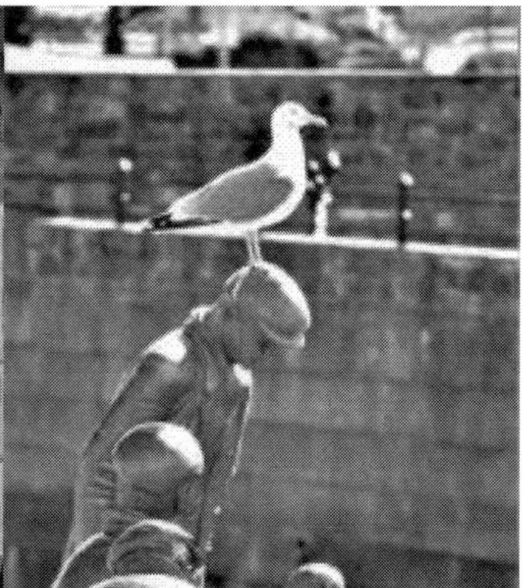

DAY 36

Sunday 3rd May 2020

Boris Johnson reveals that it was 50/50 whether or not he went on a ventilator during his miraculously short-lived hospital encounter with Coronavirus. He did not, however, say whether or not the coin-toss was a 'best of three'.

Our beloved PM and his fiancee have named their baby son Wilfred. Boris appears to have tried to give the naming of another fruit of his loins some political mileage by giving him the middle name Nicholas - apparently he had two doctors named Nick attend to him during his aforementioned hospitalisation. Nick, Nick? He could have at least shown more imagination and called it Jim Davidson!

(Pause for tumbleweed to blow across a deserted highway)

I do something a little different today in terms of Worldometer's Coronavirus statistics.

UK Coronavirus Rankings:
Total Cases: 4th highest
Total Deaths: 3rd highest
Total Tests: 7th highest
Cases per 1M population: 19th highest
Deaths per 1M population: 6th highest
Tests per 1M population: 50th highest

USA Coronavirus Rankings:
Total Cases: 1st highest
Total Deaths: 1st highest
Total Tests: 1st highest
Cases per 1M population: 14th highest
Deaths per 1M population: 14th highest
Tests per 1M population: 43rd highest

Germany Coronavirus Rankings:
Total Cases: 6th highest
Total Deaths: 7th highest
Total Tests: 3rd highest
Cases per 1M population: 29th highest
Deaths per 1M population: 23rd highest
Tests per 1M population: 30th highest

Spain Coronavirus Rankings:
Total Cases: 2nd highest
Total Deaths: 4th highest
Total Tests: 5th highest
Cases per 1M population: 6th highest
Deaths per 1M population: 4th highest
Tests per 1M population: 23rd highest

Italy Coronavirus Rankings:
Total Cases: 3rd highest
Total Deaths: 2nd highest
Total Tests: 4th highest
Cases per 1M population: 15th highest
Deaths per 1M population: 5th highest
Tests per 1M population: 20th highest

Today's Coronavirus briefing is hugely exciting. I lied. It's being given by Michael Gove, a weasel of a man, not to my liking - much like the rest of his colleagues. We hear from him that yesterday's testing figures were well below the 100,000 target - they are less than

80,000 even. Surprise, surprise! He passes to someone else who is equally dull and I switch off. Apparently there are changes afoot - they may have been announced yesterday. I think we are to be allowed more than one exercise trip outside per day. Ed aside possibly, we are unlikely to take that offer up in this household as we rarely go out once per day anyway.

I have accepted a Scrabble re-match invitation from Laura for later this evening - she is after revenge. I look forward to 'whooping her ass' again!

Ha! Ha! The joke's on me! Beth joined us for Scrabble and I came last! Laura was victorious. I'll never hear the last of it! She tells me that it's the first time she's ever beaten me.

Meanwhile Ed has been up in his room playing Trivial Pursuit with his mates online via Zoom.

My final act of the day is to respond to my employer via email. I can respond with one of three choices: A for Yes / immediate start, B for Undecided / maybe later or C for No.

I select B as I would like to know more details before deciding whether or not to do the work.

Photos on Pages 82-84 were taken on Saturday, 2nd May 2020, in Maryport.

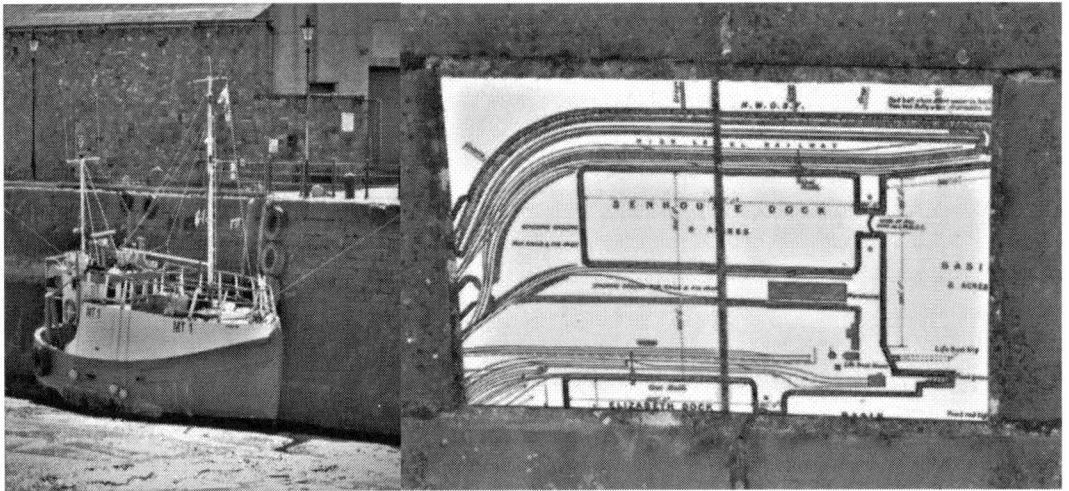

DAY 37

Monday 4th May 2020

Today would normally be a Bank Holiday in the UK, but that had already been moved to Friday 8th May to commemorate VE Day - the end of World War Two - seventy-five years ago.

Work rang me whilst I was still in bed to discuss their offer of work. I had expressed reservations about the nature of the work and we agreed that I would not be involved for now due to health issues that may have caused concerns were I to have contracted Coronavirus - that and a warning light that had come up on my car saying the engine may be damaged unless it gets serviced as soon as possible!

I sold a couple of items on eBay over the weekend, so I made another Post Office trip today. Sales have picked up quite a bit of late - it had been very quiet for months and I'd been having to relist some items five or six times. I buy and sell guitars occasionally and have been selling items I bought years ago for my hobbies that I no longer use.

I also spend an hour or so tidying up the outhouse - or annexe as Laura calls it! - so Ed can get his bike in and out a bit easier and we can find what we go looking for in there a bit more often. I manage to get soaked when I dislodge a bit of wood I'd stacked and it falls on a tap - plumbing for a washing-machine - and it sends a torrent of water shooting up at me! It's far from tidy when I eventually finish, but it's a bit better than it was and Ed's bike does go in and out easier.

DAY 38

Tuesday 5th May 2020

I awake to controversy - at least it is to my mind. Apparently UK deaths from Coronavirus are now the worst in Europe. They are now over 30,000 or 32,000 - depending on which figures you believe to be the correct or official ones. Worldometer (my 'bible' thus far), however, has them at a number still beginning with 28 thousand!

The Scottish daily virus briefing suggests that lockdown will be further extended throughout the UK for the foreseeable future. Although it looks likely that the lockdown may be relaxed earlier if there is an opportunity to do that within (the usual) three weeks.

Today feels very much like a Saturday used to feel like and I have to constantly remind myself that it isn't a Saturday and it is, in fact, a Tuesday. I look in the mirror and it says 4 p.m. - that's half-time in the football on a Saturday I tell myself, but today is a Tuesday and most Tuesdays don't have half-times, certainly not 4 p.m. ones.

I've been doing some work at the front of the house. I was so brave I didn't even wear a hat to hide my bald pate. I say bald, but there is a very short covering of hair across my head. I am impressed that there are no actual bald patches, even though I thought my hair was thinning slightly - not a lot, as Laura was insisting. Although I suspect some may not grow back as quickly, thus creating a false impression that my hair may be thinning. My hair is not thinning - ever!

I have secured into the ground a short fence section, to retain a shrub border that is currently overhanging the path that leads round the side of our house, from the front door to the front of the house. I have watered the tubs. I have cut back the road-facing side of a fuchsia bush that overhangs the pavement at the front of our property. I have pulled out weeds at the base of our front wall. I have done a lot of gathering and a bit of sweeping. In order to barrow the unwanted greenery I had to untip the wheelbarrow's contents of rocks and stones and move these by hand to the front of the house. That all requires sufficient effort to reward myself by sitting down and enjoying a can of *Desperados* in the sunshine. I hope that Laura and Ed will notice a difference my efforts have made - however small - when they return from the 'weekly shop' at the supermarket. As I sit and type some of this I wonder what the 'weekly shop' will contain apart from lots of items that Ed has chosen. I wonder if there'll be any treats for me or just Ed, the helper. I suspect they'll still need assistance coming up the steps from Laura's car with all the bags and I may not be able to escape this. I can only hope that they are so impressed with my work on the front that they only call on Beth for assistance, thinking that I will be totally exhausted from all my efforts!

We learn that Professor Neil Ferguson, sometime of Whitehaven and an epidemiologist and senior government advisor, of '250,000 UK deaths forecast' fame, has resigned over illicit visits to his home by a lady said to be in an 'open marriage'.
You couldn't make it up!

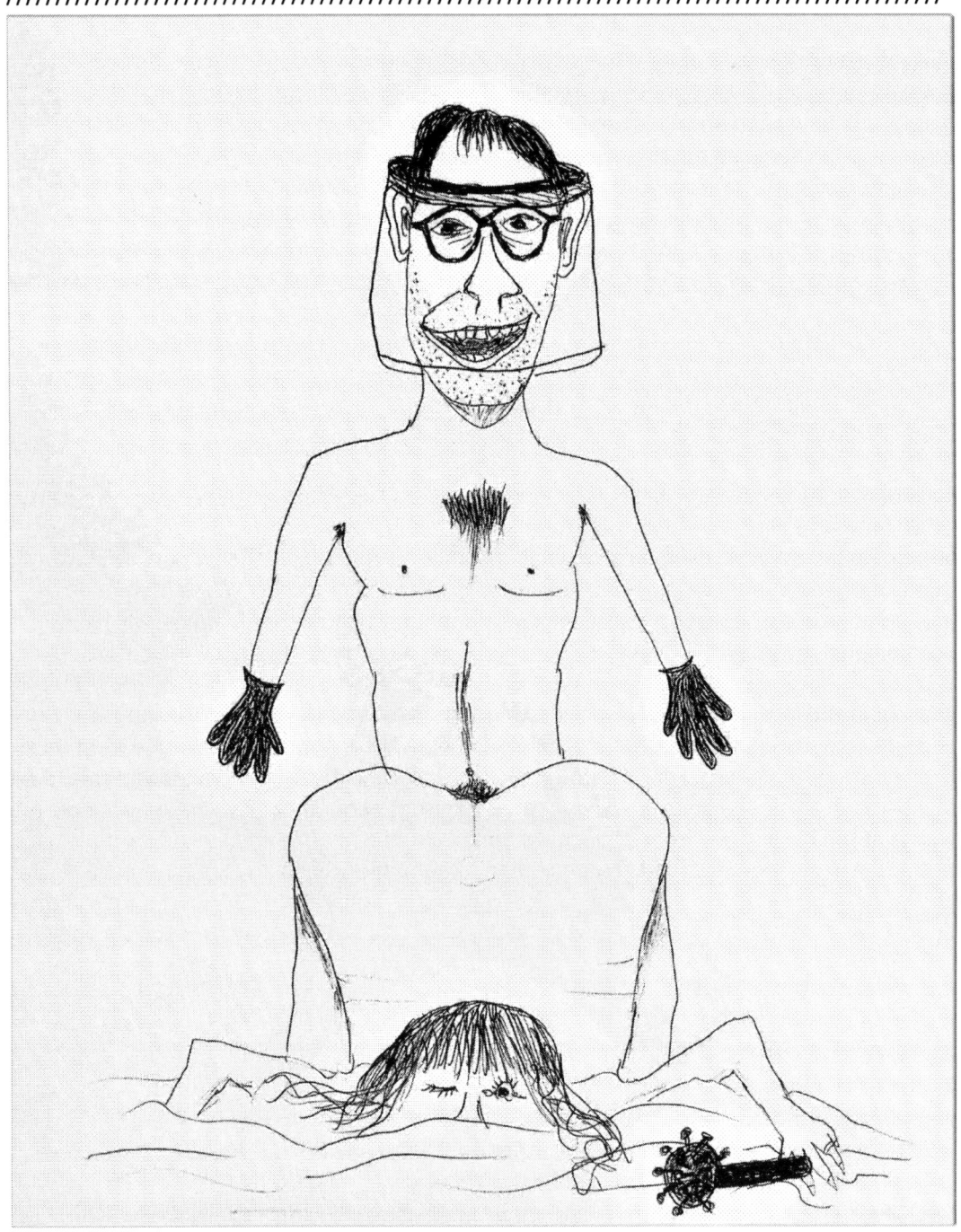

\\
STAY AT HOME > PROTECT THE NHS > SAVE LIVES > STAY AT HOME > PROTECT THE NHS > SA
//

//
VE LIVES < STAY AT HOME < PROTECT THE NHS < SAVE LIVES < STAY AT HOME < PROTECT TH
\\

DAY 39

Wednesday 6th May 2020

I take Beth breakfast up at lunch-time - a cup of tea and 3 vegetarian sausages in toasted bread with butter on two slices and tomato sauce on two slices. This is the household's preferred breakfast sandwich-making formula of late. I took Ed brekkie in bed a few days ago when I was cooking pork sausages, so this is me evening things out with the veggie!

I do a bit more work in the front garden. I would like to have done a bit more, but I couldn't be bothered to - though I can see a bit more clearly the scale of the task ahead now and it won't be anything like presentable in just a couple of days.

I pick some of the many bluebells we have growing in the front garden and give them to the girls - Laura got a couple of vases and I tied some string lightly around the stems and arranged them and everything!

The TV news reports that the pandemic has done a world of good to the environment and has done years of help to help combat climate change - I missed much of it, but think it mentioned pollution levels being the lowest for 30 years somewhere.

I catch up on the news online and hear that Boris has signalled that some lockdown measures may be eased on Monday and that the target for testing is to be increased from 100,000 to 200,000 per day by the end of the month - that could be considered quite surprising since we've only hit the last one twice and failed to hit it for the last four!

It is hinted that Boris will be letting us make multiple trips per day from Monday and allowing picnics and sunbathing. The timing of this is a bit strange when we now have more deaths than any other country in Europe, have the second most deaths world-wide and today's death total increases by 649 to 30,076.

Another milestone is passed and it gets easier to forget that each number represents a person's life taken and a grieving family.

I post the following on my Facebook page:

It's Day 39 of my Coronavirus diary today and it's getting more difficult to motivate myself to write something with each passing day. I had a chance to go back to work this week, but it would involve doorstep interviews and collecting swabs from self-administering households and I didn't fancy doing that at this stage of the pandemic, although it would have been nice to have made a contribution to helping during the crisis.

Reeni: In this some of the most important contributions will be those who stayed home, stayed back and let be.

DAY 40

Thursday 7th May 2020

"Forty days and forty nights, Thou wast fasting in the wild".

Disregarding the fact that lockdown started a little over forty days ago, the number 40 is mentioned 157 times in The Bible. It represents a period of trial, probation, testing or chastisement. It is generally accepted that the number 40 simply means 'a really long time' and should not be taken too literally.

It wouldn't surprise me if 100-year old Captain Tom - now Colonel Tom - raises forty million pounds for the NHS. As I type his current total is £32,796,275. He is all over the TV today.

We open the front door this morning to discover a red candle in a can has been left on our doorstep by a mystery visitor. Beth contacts her school friends, but none of them have left it. Maybe it's a witch's curse or a hex or a kindly gesture by a well-meaning person related to VE day anniversary celebrations.

I post the following to my Facebook page:

On the eve of the 75th anniversary of V.E. Day, I wonder how a fictitious ex-squaddie and his wife may be getting on 40-odd days into the pandemic. I wrote this poem about them before the last election. Some of you may not like it and it does contain swearing. I read it with northern accents, but any accent will do.

ON THE EVE

(HER:) "On the Eve of Christmas, we preparations make.
We cook the 'turkey-chicken' thing, some good friends small presents take.
We used to pour a glass of sherry and do a little spread on a plate.
For imaginary night-time visitors to our run-down Estate,
A carrot and a cheap mince pie will now usually suffice.
And for our tee-total Santa a glass of milk works nice.
When they're a-bed, I arrange their presents for which I scrimp and save.
I've got two little part-time jobs now - and I'm their full-time slave!
I sometimes go down the food bank - but I'm not supposed to - you see
Plenty of folk round here who are far worse off than me.
But they're alright with me, they know I've got kids to feed - three.
Three kids, two with him - he don't work, he's got PTSD.
But I manage, we get by.
For the sake of the kids I have to.
I manage and we get by."

(HIM:) "On the eve of Active Service, you think you're fully prepared,
But nothing can prepare you really, you're actually quite scared

And excited too - the adrenalin rush and the fear never fully fades.
'Cos training's only blanks fired at you - not like when you're doing raids
And live bullets crack and whizz past your ear. Or when they hit and wound your muckers.
Or they step on a mine and they're blown to bits - boom! - the poor fuckers.
They lost quite a few and we lost a few limbs, but only one dead of ours that I've seen.
They can never prepare you for that though and some of the places I've been.
And they never prepare you for when you leave and return to civvy life.
The flashbacks, the tantrums, the rows over drink and drugs with the wife.
The nightmare sleeps and the fights to free the unwelcome, irrational rage
With random lads that looked at me funny, barely half my age.
But I managed, I got through it.
And for the sake of the kids she had to.
She managed and we got through it."

(HIM:) "On the eve of the Election, I'm not sure if I'll vote.
They're all just a bunch of wankers really. But she will, she'll vote."
(HER:) "He seldom votes, which is just as well, he was Tory through-and-through.
He thinks they're for the working man, he hasn't got a clue.
My mum's family's always been Labour - well 'til Blair's weapons of mass destruction.
His dad was in the army then. My dad? He buggered off, he were into seduction.
My fella's not too bad now. I know the tours were rough
And they have scarred him mentally, the first eighteen months were tough.
But he's got so much better now, he's really calmed down a lot.
He paints. He doesn't go out much now, and he never touches a drop.
Oh, he sometimes smokes weed to numb the pain, but it's not what you'd call a habit.
And we've had no more run-ins with the police since the incident with next-door's rabbit.
(laughs)
Sometimes you have to laugh, to help you get by.
And for the sake of the kids we have to.
We do, we laugh about it now. And we manage, we get by."

(HER cont'd:) "And he no longer likes (thumbs up) those Union Jack posts - he's seen through the red, white and blue.
He had mates of all creeds and colours in t'army and he's no fan of that Tommy too."
(HIM:) "And for what it's worth, I don't like that Farage and all of his Brexit crowd.
Yes, I've served in the army like a few of them have, but that stuff don't make me feel so proud."
(HER:) "And we hate it when war and remembrance are used to feed that bloody lot's agenda.
We've lasses from all over at care home where I work, without them we wouldn't win tender.
And our Maisie's best mate's from Slovenia! I just thought that I'd throw that your way.
I'm not sure if that's even relevant, but you know what we're trying to say.
And if our Nathan fell for a Muslim lass, a Hindu, a Sikh or a Jew
It really wouldn't bother me. Or if he fell for a Polish boy too!
I'm just wanting us all to get along, and for things to just improve a bit for us lot round here.

But in cold church halls on Thursday night, we'll mark an 'X' beside vain hope I fear.
And I wonder if we'll all manage, to get by and get through?"
(HIM:) "For the sake of the kids we'll have to, love."
(HER:) "But will we though? I'd like think we'll be OK, but I'm worried'- really worried if the Tories get in. Aren't you?"

I dedicate the above poem to any ex-soldier in 'Bangla' who may be suffering from PTSD.

Dominic Raab fronts the Government's daily press conference. He dismisses claims plastered all over right-wing newspapers that an easing of the lockdown will begin on Monday as pure speculation. The papers claim to reveal some of the details of what Boris Johnson will be announcing on Sunday. I don't know if this is signalling a U-turn or merely suggesting that the Government would never dream of leaking privileged information to a fawning press. Either way, the British government is doing little to avoid attracting global criticism for its complacent Covid-19 response.

The 'R' figure, Raab informs us, is between 0.5 and 0.9 - the 0.9 figure is said (somewhat dismissively?) to be driven purely by care home stats. However, one of the Government experts alongside him references a report that suggests the 'R' has actually increased again and is now thought to be between 0.75 and the dreaded 1.0 figure. An easing of the lockdown in such circumstances - with tomorrow's planned street parties and a much-increased potential for social-distancing breaches thanks to the aforementioned newspaper reports - could be considered highly reckless, plainly stupid in fact.

Boris has always stressed the importance of avoiding a second spike, which would be absolutely disastrous for the economy as well as increasing the likelihood of more deaths on a large scale. The leaders of Scotland and Wales are worried. Other countries across the globe are watching in bewilderment and are worried for us. I think we should all be very worried about what Boris may announce on Sunday.

I go out to clap for the NHS tonight, but it is more because I really want to have a go at Boris. I shout "Up the NHS, down with Boris!" and tell the lady next door I can't be done with him. I did not dare show off the poster I had made earlier - that was purely to amuse Laura and to let off steam! The lady next door informs me that the street is having a party tomorrow and that fireworks will be let off!

DAY 41

Friday 8th May 2020

Today is the 75th Anniversary of the end of war in Europe - Victory in Europe (or VE) Day.

Days like these are always difficult for me as a pacifist. There are no winners in war as far as I am concerned and today is more about remembering all war dead than it is about celebrating anything.

I find I am getting less and less 'patriotic' as I get older. No-one in this household has any interest in displaying bunting or flying a Union Jack, but we don't have a problem with anyone who does - it's just not our thing. Personally, I have fallen out of love with our nation's flag due to its heavy usage (or abuse) by right-wing groups. I certainly don't have a problem with flags during Olympics competitions or international football matches etc. I just hate the symbol being used to push a political agenda.

After breakfast I switch on the BBC News to watch the two minutes silence and the wreath-laying by Prince Charles and (insert Royal title here) Camilla at Balmoral.

Laura drives to Allonby in the afternoon and we park up in a car park beside the only other car there; we walk along the water's edge, then back through the village. I had intended to photograph a painting of Captain Tom that I knew had appeared on the side of one of the pubs, but they also had a message painted asking for donations in return for photographs and neither of us had any cash on us and as I'm a stickler for obeying rules, I was disappointed on that front. There were people sat on picnic benches outside the pub, so it was maybe just as well I didn't start snapping!

The four of us sat outside at home with drinks and nibbles and played Scrabble for a couple of hours to try and join in the carnival spirit, but there wasn't much going on. Next door made up for our lack of flags with three Union Jacks on display and war-time music playing. The odd DIY enthusiast busied themselves and a builder carried on building in his garden, seemingly oblivious to me regaining my Scrabble crown and the gravity of the day.

Worldometer's latest Coronavirus figures are sobering.

Most New Coronavirus Deaths:
USA - 955 (so far); UK - 626; Brazil - 412; Mexico - 257; Italy - 243;
France - 243; Spain - 229; Sweden - 135; Belgium - 106; Russia - 98

Most Deaths per 1M Population (where total deaths are 50+):
Belgium - 735; Spain - 562; Italy - 500; UK - 460; France - 402;
Sweden - 314; Netherlands - 313; Ireland - 289; USA - 235; Switzerland - 209

Photos on pages 90 and pages 92 - 95 were taken in or near Allonby on 8/5/20

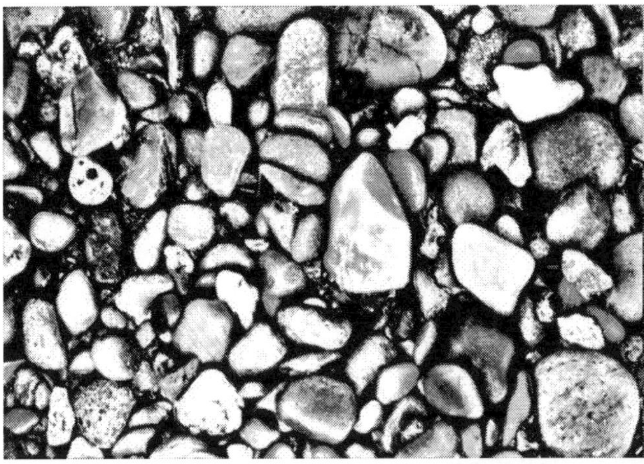

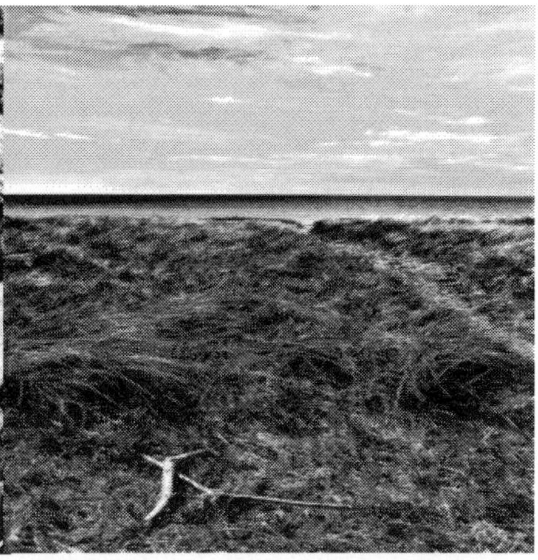

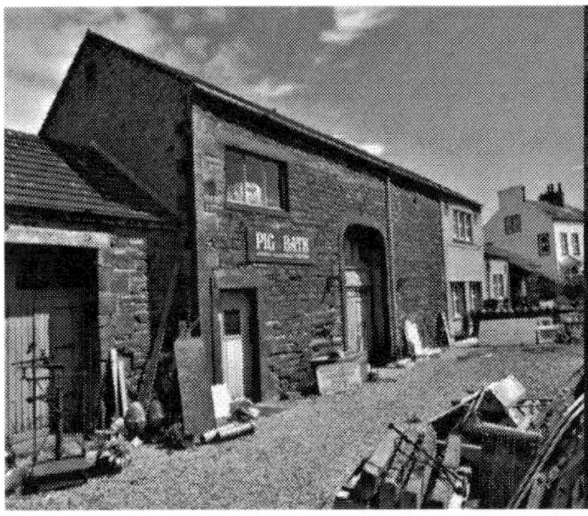

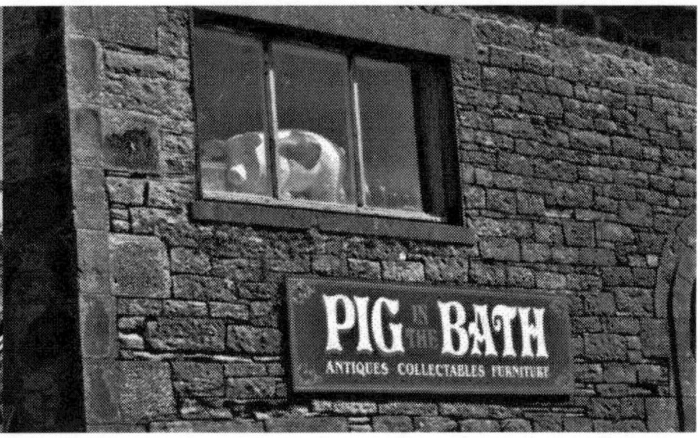

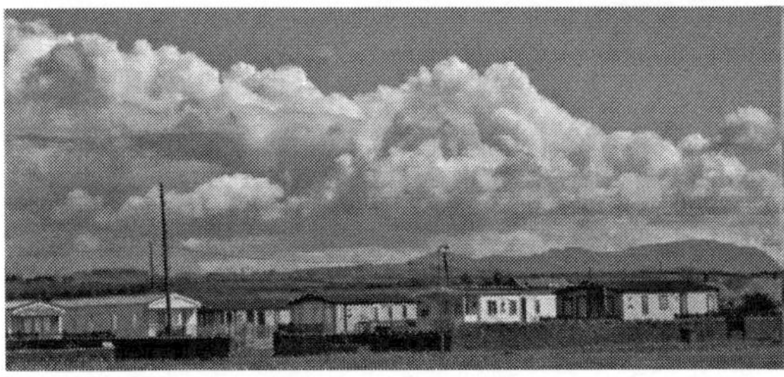

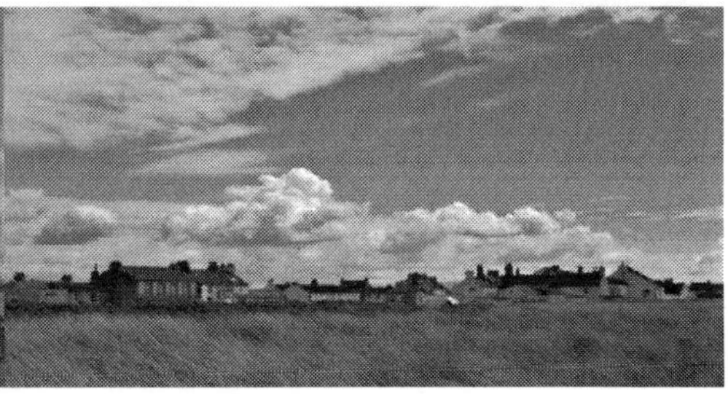

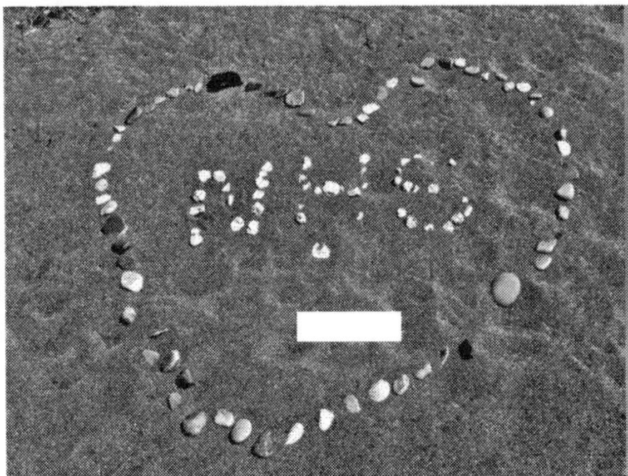

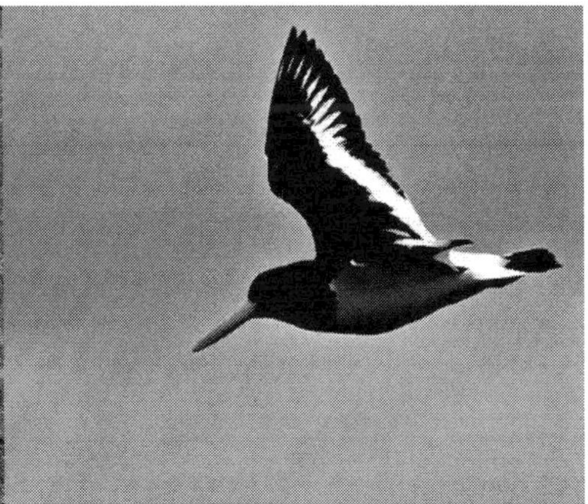

93

Photos on Pages 92-95 were taken in or near Allonby on 8/5/20

THE LAKES REMEMBER (Excerpt)

You have moved mountains to tears.
Gushing streams cascade down craggy rocks.
Slate-faced Cathedrals rise up through morning mist.
Tall sycamores bow in reverence.
The quietly incessant breeze rattles their leaves
Down through the valleys to an ocean of grief
Where the silent swell ebbs far and wide.

DAY 42

Saturday 9th May 2020

This is the end of Week 6 of keeping this diary.

I refer back to my diary at the end of Week 1.

Yes, this project has been a diversion, but it's maybe made me more focussed and kept me disciplined - something to which I am relatively unaccustomed these days. Yes, it did help me drastically reduce time spent researching and privately discussing this virus with a few of you. There are still unanswered questions, but I have not forgotten what I have learnt. My family and I are coping well. We can handle a further extension to the lockdown without any difficulty. The country is paying a price for what hasn't been done or hasn't been done well. We anxiously await what Boris is going to announce on Sunday. We will have a better idea of where we are and where we are going then.

I don't have as much frustration now. I am enjoying keeping this diary sometimes - other times it's more of a struggle, a chore. I am listening to loads more music than I usually do and doing my photography more regularly. I haven't been as inspired to write poetry as I thought I would be, but I've been reading a little bit more of it - although I haven't got round to adding some of the work I've selected for my diary to it yet. Aside from my aching right hip and knee, I'm feeling well and well rested - though prone to feeling tired, for no apparent reason, on occasion.

I have continued to keep this diary off-line, as promised, but I am still posting fairly regularly on Facebook - although I have been consciously trying to avoid giving my opinion - and I do still like to post some of the photos taken whenever I go out for a walk. If anyone has been reading this (hard-copy?) diary thus far, then I do thank you for putting up with me and my crazy ramblings. I dearly hope you and your families survived the pandemic.

I think this may be a notional half-way point along this journey. See you at the end!

END OF PART ONE

INTERLUDE

*I took this photo on 12th March 2020. A cropped version was used for the front cover.
On the same day, Boris Johnson chaired a meeting of the Government's emergency response committee, then delivered a speech which was broadcast live to the nation. It included the following extract: "The most important task will be to protect our elderly and most vulnerable people during the peak weeks when there is the maximum risk of exposure to the disease and when the NHS will be under the most pressure."*

I took this photo in Workington on 23rd March 2020 - the day lockdown was introduced.

The photo above and the top photo on Page 98 are black-and-white versions of two of the colour photos on the back cover of the book. They were taken in a Covid-free Maryport on 22nd October 2019.

MARYPORT - 12/3/20

PART TWO

> ...population became infected was right and the UK developed "herd immunity".
>
> At a private engagement at the end of February, Cummings outlined the government's strategy. Those present say it was "herd immunity, protect the economy and if that means some pensioners die, too bad".
>
> At the Sage meeting on March 12, a moment now dubbed the "Domoscene conversion", Cummings changed his mind. In this "penny-drop moment", he realised he had helped set a course for catastrophe. Until this point, the rise in British infections had been below the European average. Now they were above...

A photo of a newspaper clipping - original source unknown when sent to me by a friend.

DAY 43

Sunday 10th May 2020

I briefly jolt into action this morning with a bold Facebook post:
Governments save billions when old people die in huge numbers. I'm sure that's why no action was taken to prevent just that in 2017-18.

I add this comment:
This time it's just by taking too little action, too late. Only taking action this time due to peer pressure and it not being *just* old people dying from Covid-19.

I post it with the snapshot of (what I later find out to be) a *Sunday Times* article excerpt, sent to me by a friend:

At a private engagement at the end of February, Cummings outlined the government's strategy. Those present say it was "herd immunity, protect the economy and if that means some pensioners die, too bad".
At the Sage meeting on March 12, a moment now dubbed the "Domescene conversion", Cummings changed his mind. In this "penny-drop moment", he realised he had helped set a course for catastrophe.
<end>

I say that Dominic Cummings is the hideous face of Government without its Mr. Blobby suit on.

Mr. Blobby has a ten-minute slot on BBC 1 at 7 p.m. to make an announcement.

Beth played a game of Scrabble with me this afternoon and then four games of Frustration. I helped her to beat me at Scrabble in the closing stages of a tight encounter. It was well worth it to see how over-joyed she was to have beaten me. I clinch the final game of Frustration though to win 3-2 overall.

New Coronavirus daily death figures in most of Europe continue to reduce, but the UK still has the most daily and total deaths there. USA and, somewhat surprisingly, Ecuador fill the top two positions world-wide, with the UK lying third.

Boris Johnson faultlessly delivers what very much looks like a pre-recorded message. The main change in England will be that we can exercise outdoors as much as we like from Wednesday. He tells us to return to work if we can't work from home, but not to use public transport. This is, of course, much easier said than done!

He has a new slogan for us:

Stay Alert. Control The Virus. Save Lives.

DAY 44

Monday 11th May 2020

I had a highly significant or symbolic dream last night, but it disappeared from memory virtually the instant it ended - I only remember that it was a powerful one.

I wake up in a land of confusion.

A land in which there are more questions than answers.

The Tory Cabinet can't even agree on what Boris's announcement means. What hope is there for anyone that actually votes for them?

Meanwhile, many Boris fans among the general public are quick to defend him and offer lengthy explanations of what Boris actually meant, but which he either omitted to say or said so confusingly badly, that it could be interpreted in various ways.

Scotland has got it right, for me - far more cautious - and Nicola Sturgeon gives her usual clear, detailed, but relatively concise and unambiguous message. Not for the first time, I wish the border could be re-drawn south of Penrith.

We do get some more clarity in Parliament throughout today and some changes that we were led to believe (by the PM) would be starting today are not, in fact, starting until Wednesday. There is still much uncertainty and much to do in terms of a return to work (wherever possible and whenever it cannot be done from home).

The response to the performance of the PM at the latest virus press conference was very mixed. Taking far too long to answer relatively easy questions due to his waffling and continual employment of time-wasting tactics, there was not time for many. Our lasting memory is of Pooja - a lady whose name Boris repeated so many times it was trending on Twitter. She asked a testing question and I think it was either a bizarre way of punishing her or of scoring some imaginary brownie points with ethnic minorities.

There is now some doubt, unfortunately, as to whether or not Ed and his girlfriend will still be together (apart) by the time lockdown ends.

DAY 45

Tuesday 12th May 2020

Today is cold, dank and grey. I'm depressed.

The news is depressing, but the BBC News is more upbeat because the weekly Coronavirus death total has gone down (by c.25%) for the first time.

The Guardian tells us that the ONS figures show the true death toll is actually now over 40,000.

The weather improves and we enjoy another sunny afternoon.

Rishi Sunak, The Chancellor, brings a ray of sunshine too with his announcement that the furlough scheme is being extended until the end of July in its current form and until October with some modifications (which I won't go into now).

The daily death toll from Coronavirus in the UK compared to the rest of Europe and The World is somewhat at odds with the actions the government is beginning to take (to get us back to work) and the better news on the weekly total.

A personal disappointment is hearing that Matt Hancock said on morning TV that people are unlikely to be going on foreign holidays at all this Summer. It looks like our July holiday will be going the same way as our April one.

DAY 46

Wednesday 13th May 2020

I get up very late and grumpy. I don't feel my best - my SUNCT headache syndrome has been visiting me, but thankfully the attacks are not as painful as they can be. I take it out on the kids by criticising the various examples of laziness they have demonstrated this morning, in my sternest, shouty voice.

There is less need to be *so* lazy when we have a lot more time on our hands than usual; time to secure the gate properly after putting your bike away; time to flush a chain and put the toilet lid down or to put a loaf back in the bread bin - and time to put a surplus slice of bread back in the bag and not on top of the aforementioned loaf.

Petty, I know. I feel guilty almost immediately and I can tell and understand why everyone is unhappy with me to varying degrees. There will be time to make it up to them and time to forgive.

Today you can play golf if you have the time. Golf, tennis, football, basketball - any sport as long as there's only two of you playing the game and you keep two metres apart.

494 new UK Coronavirus deaths (and over 3,000 new cases) are announced today. We are nearing 500 deaths per 1M population. UK is outside the top 30 countries in terms of Testing per 1M population rankings. Source: Worldometer - 15.50 13/5/20

At 8 p.m. I joined 'Poets Out Loud meets Speakeasy' via Zoom for a couple of hours of poetry, prose - and even some musical contributions!

I will let our host and facilitator, Philip Hewitson, give you a flavour of the evening:

"SpeakEasy met up with Poets Out Loud again on zoom last night for a wonderful evening of sharing, words and music, sunsets and silliness.

There were Haiku galore, several sonnets, a sestina and a plethora of limericks, some even specially dedicated (I was thrilled! So was Annie!). New books were promoted, we recalled a display of bent books and heard a song about a bookmark in our hearts.

We took a walk on a May morning, admired the greenery, nature carrying on and the silence broken by birdsong. We marvelled at a lemon meringue sky, took a journey up Lakeland's mountains to visit the kings of our county, but could it be a step too far? Luckily avoiding an avalanche of unicorns was some top advice.

Unfinished poems discovered they might be complete after all these years, recalling joy and pain, the Lakes remembered in the summer rain. To make matters verse it got very deep when we wondered does a leaf know where it will go, is it aware of its fate?

'Can we endure isolation?' we asked, and took care to avoid the covidiot driver taking a spin around a care home. Walking the damn dog gave the wrong impression, our tour round a virtual museum exhibition by a post-impressionist inspired us, and we found ourselves entering the corona-verse! Who was the man who changed what was right to what was right? We hoped people won't flood into the Lake District and put pressure on our Health Care. We took time to remember and paid tribute to Cumbrian victims of COVID 19.

Home-made masks appeared as it was learned just how busy we've been in lockdown, remember only boring people get bored! Busy but not lonely. And I know it's not forever, we can all play our part, but here is where the madness lies and most importantly "are you not wearing pants?" (Someone is allergic to elastic!)

For now we sit and watch the world, enjoy the silence and hope that in the end, perhaps, we will be wiser.

Keep safe and well, hopefully see you again next time!!"

....

SUMMER RAIN

Oh how I long for Summer rain
And to remember a time when we held hands
And ran barefoot through puddles
And stinging nettles again!

Made paper boats out of discarded poetry
We wished we'd kept once the ink had run
And fished them out with sticks that dogs had tired of
And left them to dry in the evening sun.

DAY 47

Thursday 14th May 2020

Shared a couple of photos that I 'stole' and enlarged of Dalston Amateur Rugby League Club with me, middle row, second from left in red-and-black kit.

1983 we think, after a couple of shares, a few comments and some likes.

Cleared and flattened some ground at the front of the house.

Built a rough, low, short retaining wall next to it, using some large rocks.

Wheel-barrowed about ten bags of topsoil and sand and gravel - bought over two years ago - from the side of the house to the front and spread them over the ground next to the retaining wall.

Raked and levelled the mix and tamped it down.

Had dinner with Ed and Laura and watched one episode of Season 6 of *60 Days Inside* by mistake after I clicked on a link Ed sent me.

Ed had to link up my laptop to the TV for us to watch it on some (illegal?) site. That probably explains the ads for porn sites that kept flashing up in the top left corner of the screen.

We watched the first episode of Season 2 of *60 Days Inside* until it became too stop-start due to buffering (?) to continue.

I listened to a live improvised 57 minute session 'behind closed doors' by Thorsten Quaeschning of Tangerine Dream (+ guest) from Berlin through headphones on my laptop whilst Laura watched TV.

Mr. Q's guest had some very unusual instruments to add to the usual electronics. It was a stunning rhythmical masterpiece and sublimely beautiful.

I played Scrabble afterwards with Beth. She brought the box to me and sat down next to me. I didn't have the heart to decline.

Time with Beth is special.

Laura brought us drinks and snacks. There was much laughter. I enjoyed it.

Beth was happy. She played well. I won. And she was *still* happy!

DAY 48

Friday 15th May 2020

I get fed up very easily when I come across lies and hypocrisy. I have been coming across Facebook posts on a similar theme - with subtle differences here and there - portraying Boris Johnson as a near-broken man, a man who is only trying to do his very best for the country in difficult circumstances and asking us to be kind and supportive of him. They usually start with "this is not a political post" - when they clearly are - and may say "whether you love him or loathe him" and usually mention Caroline Flack (a celebrity who received online abuse and subsequently committed suicide). Usually these posts are accompanied by a photograph of Boris looking like a near-broken man.

These posts look like the stage-managed works of a brilliant PR team - ones that would stoop to any level imaginable to achieve a desired result - whether that be daubing shit on a bus to achieve an unlikely EU referendum outcome or pulling off a sensational General Election victory for a serial liar.

I suggest that the people who have been unkind to Boris over TRUTHS may apologise to him when the people who absolutely slaughtered Corbyn and Abbott with LIES have done so, but everyone tends to just ignore me and I can't blame them for that - it's a lonely furrow I plough these days it seems.

Laura and I snook quickly out of the house with only the most cursory goodbye, picnic and camera in hand, to enjoy a couple of hours in Silloth - a fine example of a Victorian seaside resort (if you've amazingly never heard of it).

"Quick, before they notice!" she said. This is the furthest we have travelled since the start of lockdown. Silloth lies 13.5 miles north-east of our home. I have to drive Laura's car so I can't criticise her driving. I didn't want to drive her car - she made me do it! I have not used my car since a scary warning light came on. I won't drive it again until the day I get it sorted and serviced - I am not sure yet when that will be, but I'm in no hurry.

Somewhat ironically in these times of social-distancing, the highlight of our walk - for me, at least - was fenced off and I had to hold my camera aloft to take photos.

'Big Fella' - a metal sculpture by Durham-based steel fabricator Ray Lonsdale of a man and his dog - was a gift to the town by the late Mr. Peter Richardson and his family. The pair are sat on a wooden bench. The man shields his eyes from the late evening sun and admires the view as the dog eagerly watches the ball at its master's feet. 'Big Fella' has room beside him on the bench for folks to have their photo taken with him. But, sadly, not today.

Today we cannot get within two metres of him!

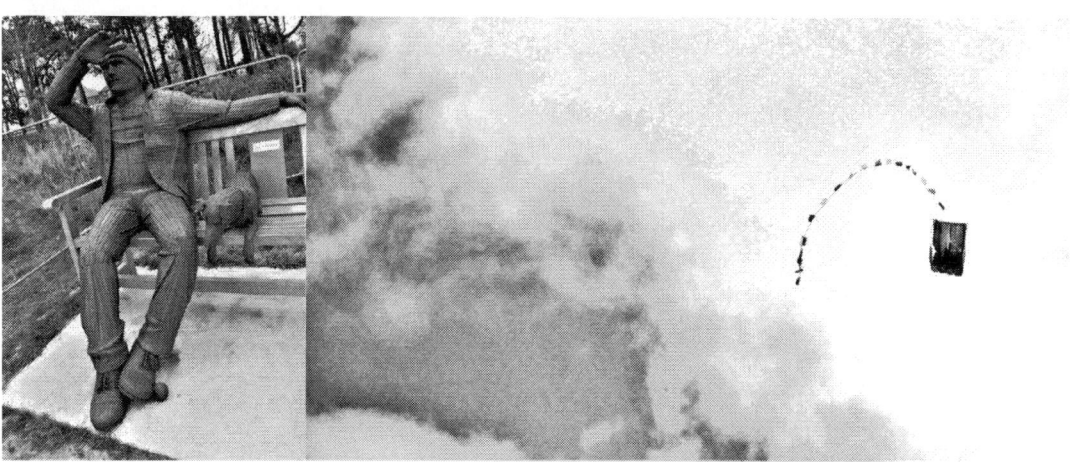

Photos on Pages 106-7 were taken in Silloth on Friday 15th May 2020.

DAY 49

Saturday 16th May 2020

Today I decide to deactivate my Facebook account for a week - knowing full well I won't manage to avoid going into it for that long.

Today I have decided that everyone hates me and it would be better if I move into an empty property I co-own, seven miles away, in Aspatria. The property is the bane of my life, *a severe drain on my finances and, on occasions where it escapes the dark recesses of my mind, a cause of depression* - but that's a story I won't go into *further*. It was not a serious suggestion, but the mere mention of it is enough to send Laura into a huff. I can't be arsed to say sorry to the required degree of sincerity demanded by her, so we may as well write off the rest of today. I go upstairs, lie alone on the matrimonial bed and listen to music as I type this.

I also make this poem from album titles by the prog rock band King Crimson:

LARKS' TONGUES IN ASPIC

In the Court of The Crimson King
Starless and Bible Black
Larks' Tongues in Aspic
Red
Lizard
Islands
Beat
The Power to Believe
In the Wake of Poseidon
Earthbound
The Great Deceiver
Absent lovers
Three of a Perfect Pair
Ladies of The Road

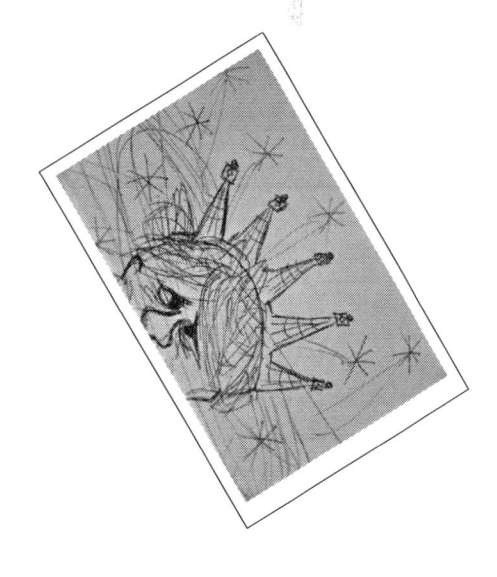

The Night Watch
Epitaph
The Construction of Light
Sleepless
Elektrik
Cirkus
Heartbeat
A Young Person's Guide to
Discipline
Frame by Frame
The Deception of The Thrush
21st Century Guide
The Projects
Radical Action to Unseat the Hold of Monkey Mind
Vroom Vroom
B'boom
Thrak
Thrakattak
Heavy Construction
Meltdown
The Elements of King Crimson

Build-A-Boris - 2022

DAY 50

Sunday 17th May 2020

I snuggle up to Laura, kiss her and whisper that I love her. She tells me that she loves me too.

That is all that matters.

It *is* all that matters and it is enough to end our childish feud.

But, alas, all is not well in the world. There are rows over easing the lockdown and a proposed return to school. There are rows and protests about the continuation of lockdown and the removal of freedoms that were previously afforded to people. You can't please all of the people all of the time at any time, so pleasing some of the people some of the time might be the best that we should hope for in a pandemic.

Living in the UK, we're probably getting a lot more freedoms than our statistics deserve, but they were much reduced today with only 170 new deaths announced. Nevertheless it is still the 4th highest worldwide.

I play two games of Scrabble with Beth today. She just comes downstairs and plonks the box down on the table near where I can usually be found sitting for hours on end. It is now expected of me to oblige her with a game or two and I am usually happy to.

The Archbishop of Canterbury has been discussing the nation's mental health and his own struggles. We are told from elsewhere that 50% of adults are currently suffering from anxiety. I wonder what the other 50% must be suffering from.

DAY 51

Monday 18th May 2020

I notice an untypical *Guardian* headline online:

"South Korean football team apologises for using sex dolls to fill stands"

Earlier in the month, the K-League were the first major national league to hold matches since the start of the pandemic. FC Seoul said the dolls had been ordered inadvertently after a "misunderstanding" with the supplier. There are concerns they may have brought the whole country into disrepute.

NoBlo BoJo Comes with own hot air.
Can be programed
he say anyhting you want.
You can ***'Buy Now, Pay Forever!'***
STRICTLY NO REFUNSD!
If when left, you be deflated.

'Deflated' - 2022

I spend an hour or so in the afternoon doing some light housework. It won out over work in the garden because the weather conditions were not absolutely perfect for heavy manual labour. I enjoy another 'behind closed doors' musical premiere from Thorsten and guest on my laptop, then a couple of games of Scrabble with Beth. The spoils shared and one happy step-daughter later, Laura joins us to watch a movie, but I give up half-way through as it fails to match its billing. I go to bed and listen to a CD.

DAY 52

Tuesday 19th May 2020

I dreamt about queueing in a bar to order a round of drinks for myself and friends, re-visiting the bar to discover two drinks I'd left on it had disappeared, getting replacement drinks, then returning to a different table from the one I'd left with half-empty glasses. On a subsequent return to the table I discover my friends had left the pub and some acquaintances - friends of friends, sat outside - invited me to join them. There was promise of a good time with live music, but I was then transported to a fictitious football game - Carlisle United hammering four goals past Mansfield at Brunton Park in a stand with a 'restricted view'. So restricted that I missed every goal. That is an excruciating thing to happen when you're a football fan. It's like the worst nightmare imaginable.

There is more football when I check Facebook. A friend has posted footage of a memorable game from the 1974-75 season - Carlisle United's only season in the top flight. Three goals in the net opposite the one my 13-year old self was stood behind. The best Carlisle team ever - despite being bottom of the league and essentially the same team promoted in the previous season - and one of the best Carlisle performances ever. Lowly Carlisle beat league-leaders Everton 3-0 and achieved the double over them at a packed Brunton Park. Despite winning 12 of their 42 games, Carlisle went on to be relegated along with Chelsea and Luton Town, Everton eventually finished 4th and it was Derby County who went on to win the League.

The BBC News headlines include the following: Easyjet have revealed hackers have accessed the personal details of around 9 million travellers, but say there is no evidence that any personal information has been misused. UK unemployment has risen by c.50,000 to 1.35M in the 3 months to March. The number of people claiming unemployment benefits has risen by over 850,000 in April - 2.1M people are now claiming. Donald Trump has confirmed he has been taking an anti-malaria drug, to ward off Covid-19, for about ten days. Northern Ireland is now letting groups of up to six people who don't live together to meet up outdoors. This is out of step with the rest of the UK - especially Scotland and Wales.

UK new Coronavirus deaths announced today are 545, taking the UK total to over 35,000. Excess deaths for March and April are reported to be c.50,000

Today I feel I am buckling somewhat under the weight of something. I do have fairly broad shoulders, but the weight of *something* has been steadily building on them over the last few days. I'm not really sure what that something is, but I'm expecting to shake it off, rather than crumble.

Maybe it's the weight of those 50,000 excess deaths in just two months.

We're hoping to have a family barbecue tomorrow - weather permitting. I *do* hope it's a sunny day!

Photos on Pages 109 & 112 were taken in Silloth on Friday 15th May 2020

Recommended Listening For Tangerine Dream:
70s 'Classics': RICOCHET, RUBYCON, ENCORE, FORCE MAJEURE
80s: TANGRAM, WHITE EAGLE, UNDERWATER SUNLIGHT, POLAND
2000s: MALA KUNIA, QUANTUM GATE, RECURRING DREAMS, THE SESSIONS II-V, RAUM
WARNING: If you're lucky, this music really could change your life!

DAY 53

Wednesday 20th May 2020

We rise late despite it being a lovely day outside - so late that Ed had returned from a long bike ride and brought up cups of tea for me and his mum.After a quick soak in the bath I walk down the hill to the (closed) local surgery and drop my repeat prescription for high blood pressure tablets through the letter-box, just to the right of the main entrance. There is no sign of life, telephone instructions had already informed me I will have to contact the pharmacy by phone on Friday to arrange how I can collect my medication. I will have run out before then - I have been rationing my pills the last few days anyway - but this is something I never get overly concerned about. Once, a long time ago, I stopped taking tablets for years. This is not a recommendation. Please don't try this at home!

The return walk, uphill, is enough to count as decent exercise and has me slightly out of breath and perspiring. Perversely, the walk uphill feels somewhat easier - the downhill walk had me limping a bit and my dodgy right knee felt more painful going down than up. I'm told the family barbecue - just the four of us - is scheduled for 4 O'Clock. This is a slightly later start than I'd have liked - but Laura is calling the shots and she wants it to be tea-time when she eats. That's also the time when our 'side terrace area', as she calls it, will receive most sun.

It's 2 p.m. as I type this and I haven't eaten anything yet today. To avoid breaking the peace I have already told Ed he can do the barbecue - arranging it, lighting it, cooking on it - as long as I can supervise. Ed was good enough, after all, to have cleaned the barbecue yesterday - albeit in an unorthodox way, using sand-paper! Supervisor, I have decided, gets to consume more alcohol than the one or two drinks (if any) I would normally have. This is the whole point - apart from doing everything al fresco - of a barbecue after all, isn't it? Drinking? If I had much hair - it's currently only about an inch long - I would be letting it down a tad later this afternoon.

DAY 54

Thursday 21st May 2020

Laura was moaning loudly during the early hours. I shook her awake from her nightmare. She had been mid-fall when she awoke. "A fall from a ceiling", she said. How did she get up there? "I don't know - some sort of supernatural force", she said.

Today was possibly the lowest we've felt as a family since the start of the pandemic.

Laura and I were both feeling down for no good reason.

Ed has been down since he and his girlfriend split up and seemed a bit more down today than on previous days. He did at least meet up with a friend for a bike ride - albeit a shorter one than usual.

Beth has been at her most 'room-bound' and did not bring the Scrabble out today.

We are a family in need of a hug, but no-one is allowed to hug us.

I struggled to find any words for today and typed all of this the following lunchtime.

DAY 55

Friday 22nd May 2020

I get up at 07.20, feed the cats, put three full wheelie-bins out and go back to bed.

It's after 11.00 when I get up and go out again and it's a very windy day - the emptied bins have fallen over and are blocking the pavement. I drag our three back up our steps, one at a time, and lift them over our locked, stomach-height side-gate - it's quicker than the alternative and counts as exercise. Then I go through the house to the back door and wheel the three bins into their usual position - up against the wall opposite our back door, next to a bolted door we virtually never use that opens onto a lane a couple of very steep half-steps below. They are the sort of steps you could probably use to help yourself mount a medium-sized horse - providing it isn't galloping - but not much use for heavy bins or anything else.

The lie-in has made me feel weary, if anything, and part of me wishes I'd stayed up. My knee and hip have been aching a little more than usual, but I may still manage some time working on the front garden.

A couple of hours later and I haven't done any work on the garden. Laura suggests we go for a walk. She drives me down to the harbour and we enjoy a short walk along the prom before diverting onto a part we had never been on together before - the North Pier, a long man-made promontory which stretches out into the sea until it's opposite the lighthouse. I do my usual photography thing as we try to avoid being blown over by the wind.

Laura stops for shopping on the way back home. She makes up a flask of tea and I butter some bread, then we set off with the kids in tow and head for Allonby for take-out fish 'n' chips.

The Codfather is very quiet. It reopened a week ago and Laura found it very easy to social-distance inside and doesn't have to wait too long before our 'cooked to order' suppers are ready. We drive to a car park a few hundred metres away, one where we can enjoy a decent view as we tuck in to our first proper meal outside our home since the lockdown began, albeit enjoyed sat in a car. It is far too windy to venture out.

We all enjoy a very different dining experience, one we've not enjoyed for a long time and it lifts everyone's spirits somewhat - especially when Laura parks up opposite Twentyman's and treats us all to an ice-cream of our choice!

As we sit opposite, eating their delicious fayre, we notice that the Twentyman's business was established one hundred years ago. That's almost twice as long as I've been visiting Allonby.

Today has been a good day.

Maryport
22/05/20

116

DAY 56

Saturday 23rd May 2020

I am first to rise. I take a bath then go down and cook breakfast for myself and the kids - Laura has already had toast. It is worth the time and the effort when I see the beaming smile on Beth's face when I take her breakfast in bed - a toasted fried egg sandwich. I do the same for Ed a few minutes later, except he's got sausage - same as I'm having.

The day is dominated by *that* news about Dominic Cummings and his family. I'm banking on this not requiring any further explanation. There *should* be enough being said and done about it over the next few days. Whether or not there is anything *done* about it remains to be seen.

DAY 57

Sunday 24th May 2020

Boris doesn't sack Cummings and Cummings doesn't resign.
It's a funny Britain we live in these days, but not in a good way.

DAY 58

Monday 25th May 2020

Today is a Bank Holiday, but that means nothing to anyone in this household in the current situation. I cannot speak for the rest of the country, but I suspect there may be many millions in the UK for whom that is the case.

Dominic Cummings is still in post. He even got over an hour of everyone's time in front of TV cameras in the garden of 10 Downing Street.

DAY 59

Tuesday 26th May 2020

I visited the Post Office to post a parcel and collected my prescription from the pharmacy today.

I presented these snapshots of where the UK currently lies globally in tackling Coronavirus:

Countries with Most Deaths per 1M population (+total deaths):
San Marino - 1,238 (42)
Belgium - 806 (9,344)
Andorra - 660 (51)
Spain - 574 (26,837)
UK - 546 (37,048)
Source: Worldometer 26/5/20 - 16.18

Coronavirus: UK has 19th most cases per 1M population, 5th most deaths per 1M population and 2nd most deaths worldwide.

UK has the 21st largest population and is outside the top 30 by density of population. <end>

Laura and I drove to Whitehaven for a stroll before supper. I don't think we've visited since last year. It was nice to see some new additions but, perhaps understandably, it looked like it was missing a bit of TLC. I put an album of photos up on Facebook after I had painstakingly removed some litter and guano (seagull poo) on my computer.

Unfortunately there is not a computer program that can help us to remove all the shit in our lives and make us less in need of some TLC.

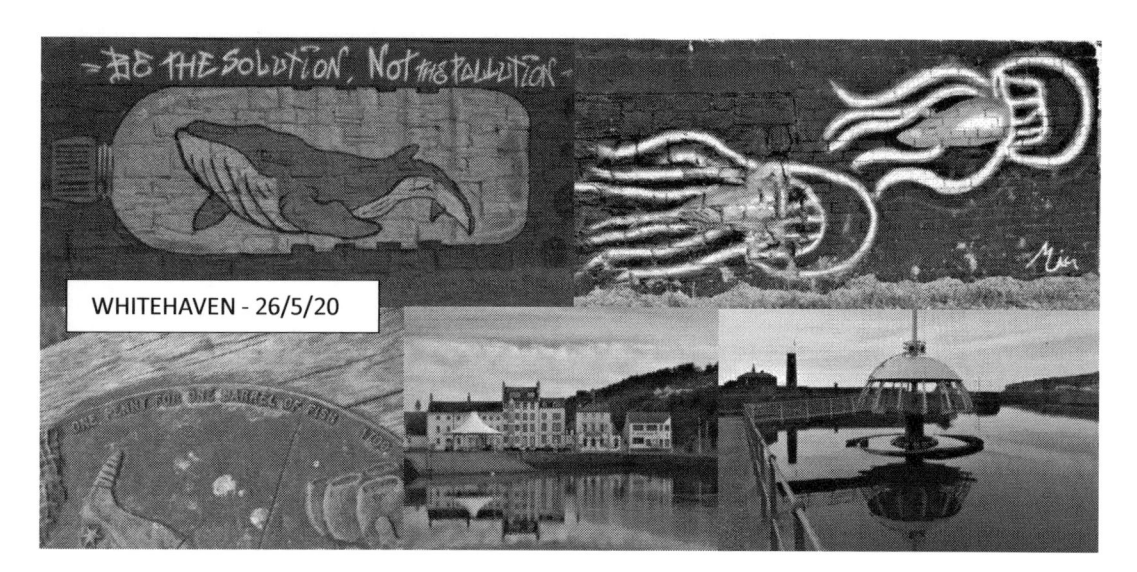

WHITEHAVEN - 26/5/20

DAY 60

Wednesday 27th May 2020

There are some concerns about Beth in the morning. She has fallen out slightly with her mum over said concerns and some harsh words being exchanged. It will turn out to be the proverbial 'storm in a tea-cup', but 'kid gloves' will be needed and there may be some 'walking on egg-shells' for a while.

Ed and I think it could be prudent to scarper and decide to finally take the old super-king-size mattress to the council 'tip'. We have to queue on the road, two corners away behind twenty other cars or so. Thank goodness they've made it one-way only into the recycling centre to eliminate potential queue-jumping. The social distancing, once inside, is exemplary - only allowing two vehicles at a time into the compound. It was much easier to remove the mattress from Laura's car than it was to get it out of the house, down the steps and (miraculously!) into the back of her little Toyota Yaris!

I accept an invitation to join the Carlisle-based poetry group, SpeakEasy, online at 7.30 p.m. I have written three poems this last week or so - quite extraordinary! - two of them (nonsense poems) for amusement purposes, one because I had something I needed to say. The first is the one constructed from King Crimson album titles on Day 49 (Page 107). These are the other two poems that I read:

SONGS, A MARS BAR ADVERT AND CASABLANCA CORRECTLY QUOTED

Lucy in the sky
With Diamonds are a girl's best
Friend of Mine eyes have

Seen the Glory Days
Like These foolish things remind
Me of You are the

Sunshine of my Life
On Mars A day helps you work
Rest and Play it, Sam

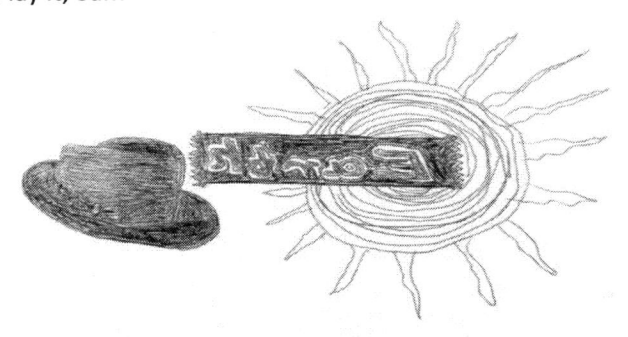

TIME TO KILL?

The clock tick-tocks more slowly now
Yet flies by in some other ways
We've spent the equivalent of six months together
In the last sixty days

The children have turned into young adults
Without the help of education
Whilst lives were rightly put on hold and cherished
Across our divided nation

I see a glimpse of your hair in time
Twelve years from now I'd say
When you no longer feel the need
To battle against the grey

And who knew you had such an extensive
Wardrobe of animal-print pyjamas?
Baggy ones with monkeys, cats and dogs
And double-headed llamas!

The make-up bag lies neglected
You don't use much, you don't need it anyway
My love for you is water-tight
I will love you always

And then there is the serious stuff
The care home deaths through lack of personal protection
And three years worth of excess deaths
In the wider population

I've been trying to avoid the politics
Since the last general election
But was the Pandemic hitting us second worst
Just our Government killing time on reflection?

....

My poems have usually been weeks, months and, sometimes, years in the making. I would not normally present rushed, 'work in progress' examples of it, but other things seem to matter much more than being seen as mildly inferior, mediocre or overly precious.

A friend and I have a brief exchange on Facebook about the Coronavirus figures - the crux of it is to do with concerns about claims of possible under-reporting in Brazil (where TV showed a burial of about 150 bodies in a mass grave in Sao Paulo) and a shared concern about the UK getting a second spike. It is most amicable.

DAY 61

Thursday 28th May 2020

Laura and I get up together - slightly earlier than of late - and enjoy breakfast and assorted news sources together. We are in fairly good spirits.

There is lots of news - I hesitate to say that it's exciting news, but there is plenty that interests me. It's quite hectic in that respect. It takes up most of my day.

SpeakEasy's video of last night's online poetry shenanigans is blocked at first when it is put on Youtube - I thought it might have been due to a poem I constructed from album titles, but it turns out it was for some brief musical content. I watch my contribution with only slight disappointment and embarrassment - I am getting more used to seeing myself do it.

New Coronavirus deaths announced so far today:

Mexico - 463
USA - 449
UK - 377
Brazil - 238
Russia - 174
India - 161
Canada - 108
Italy - 70
Iran - 63
Chile - 49

These are the 10 highest / worst numbers out of the 68 (of 215) countries who have either announced or have deaths to date.

84 countries had deaths announced yesterday.

A total of 184 countries have suffered deaths throughout the pandemic.

Source: Worldometer 28/5/20 17.29

The 'organiser' of Clap For Carers / Clap For The NHS wants tonight to be the last time we express our gratitude at 8 p.m. on Thursdays - aware that it is becoming politicised.

I use the opportunity to applaud loudly outside the back door, a sincere and sustained clap, before launching a tirade against Boris. I give him the peaceful equivalent of the proverbial 'kicking' outside the back door, then out of a window which I open especially for that purpose, and throughout the whole ground floor of the house - even the downstairs loo. My booming voice is enough to set my heart racing and, due to our location, I know it will have echoed loudly. I imagine it echoing loudly down the hill and spreading out as it goes - the sonic equivalent of a snowball. No, an avalanche or a Mexican wave.

"Boris out! Up the NHS, up the carers, down with Boris! Boris out - and take Cummings with you!"

In reality, I doubt it will have raised more than a couple of eyebrows, a few asking "who's that nutter?", one "dear me, is there any need?" and a couple of "is that him at number 9?"s. But sometimes it's good to let off steam, it's cathartic and I never tire of doing things to embarrass myself in front of Laura and the kids, who can no doubt hear me upstairs. I feel the fool I probably look to Laura, and sounded - to anyone that heard me - when my laptop tells me it is now 8.08 p.m.

Gosh, that lasted 8 minutes. How embarrassing! But, much to my surprise, Laura was quite supportive of me letting off steam and echoed my sentiments!

I feel brief guilt at hijacking the weekly ritual, but I'm sure there are many in the NHS who would rather have seen more support by way of having adequate PPE and ventilators and a much quicker lockdown in place that might have made their plight somewhat more bearable.

I am soon over it. Cathartic, I say, cathartic - in a Fred Elliott sort of way.

My outburst has, at least, given me something more to write about. It's been a massive struggle of late to contribute *anything*.

WHITEHAVEN - Tuesday, 26th May 2020

DAY 62

Friday 29th May 2020

Today would have been the 55th birthday of my friend and fellow Carlisle United fan Adrian Scott. I hope he's in a better place than this pandemic-ridden world with its crazy leaders and warring people.

Ed has been feeling down today - fed up, bored, frustrated at not being able to see his dad and grandparents who live in another county. He's normally consistent in his moods, arguably the most consistent of all of us, but we all seem to be having 'off days' - or weird mood days as I saw someone describe them - more often lately. You wouldn't realise it from his sulky mood, but he is happy to hear the news that Year 12 (his age group) are scheduled to return to school on 15th June. For Beth (Year 10) it's looking like a September return, but we seem to be edging to a phase where everything could be subject to change.

Leaked Sage documents from weeks and months ago included a warning: The entire UK population may need flu jabs in the coming winter as the search for a Covid-19 vaccine continues.
I post: Make of this whatever you will:
The entire UK population may need flu jabs in the coming winter as the search for a Covid-19 vaccine continues.
(A warning from SAGE)
Facebook friend: Never had one and never will
ME: I think I'd be much less inclined to now after researching the excess winter deaths of 2017-18 and seeing how ineffective flu vaccines can sometimes be in 'preventing death' - let's just leave it at that.
I have never been anti-vaccines previously and I am not saying that I am now either but, on balance, I may refuse one if offered. That said, I almost died myself in early 2018 (not flu-related) and I didn't have one! <end>

There are anecdotal reports that everywhere seems a lot busier than this time last week. I am becoming increasingly concerned that a second spike may be inevitable and that what many believe may be the beginning of the end, may not even be the end of the beginning.

Things that had some bearing on Excess Winter Deaths in 2017-18 being the highest since 1975-76:
A prolonged spell of extremely cold weather; influenza; the ineffectiveness of the flu vaccine; the NHS's most serious "winter crisis" for many years; lack of staff; lack of beds; health services - particularly hospitals - being unable to cope with the numbers of patients needing treatment; the severity of some patients' conditions.

You could be forgiven for thinking we had something very similar to Covid-19 in 2017-18.

<I added the info in this box to here in 2022>

DAY 63

Saturday 30th May 2020

I am glad to start the day hearing from my cousin 'down under' via Facebook that my lovely Auntie Anne - my late father's sister-in-law - is alive and well and celebrating her 80th Birthday today!

I'm up bright and early. I had to get up to put the bin out - they're a day later this week due to the Bank Holiday. The cats benefit from a rare early weekend breakfast.

I busy myself with Worldometer's Coronavirus 'key stats' from yesterday. I've decided the way below may be the best way to report my regular (but not necessarily daily) updates.

I post the following:-

Total deaths from Coronavirus as of yesterday (29/5/20):

USA - 104,542 (331)
UK - 38,161 (68)
Italy - 33,229 (60)
France - 28,714 (65)
Brazil - 27.944 (212)
Spain - 27,121 (47)
Belgium - 9,430 (12)
Mexico - 9,044 (129)
Germany - 8,594 (84)
Iran - 7,677 (84)
Worldwide - 366,422

Number in brackets is population rounded to nearest million.

New Coronavirus deaths announced yesterday:

USA - 1,212 (331)
Brazil - 1,180 (212)
Mexico - 447 (129)
UK - 324 (68)
India - 269 (1379)
Russia - 232 (146)
Peru - 131 (33)
Canada - 102 (38)
Italy - 87 (60)
Sweden - 84 (10)
Worldwide - 4,873

Number in brackets is population rounded to nearest million.

Deaths per 1M population (where total deaths are 100+) as of yesterday:

Belgium - 814 (5,012)
Spain - 580 (6,110)
UK - 562 (3,997)
Italy - 550 (3,841)
France - 440 (2,863)
Sweden - 431 (3,614)
Netherlands - 346 (2,692)
Ireland - 333 (5,043)
USA - 316 (5,421)
Switzerland - 222 (3,564)
Worldwide - 47 (773)

Number in brackets is cases per 1M population.   Source: Worldometer

I like this format and I think I will try to stick to it - time and motivation allowing. Or until I get bored with it!

I catch up with my daughter Charlotte on the phone and try my daughter Becky but there's no answer. She contacts me via FB Messenger to say she's on a bike ride (in the capital) and will ring me later. Laura makes us a coffee and joins me - the children haven't surfaced yet. It's 10.45 as I finish this sentence.

Becky does keep her promise and we enjoy a long-overdue catch-up as she takes a break from her hectic work schedule - she's a high-flying civil servant. Her 'Boris Bike' ride, as it turned out, had been an unsuccessful errand to collect a parcel delivered to her former address. We also discuss well-being, her work and (inevitably) the virus.

Later in the afternoon, Ed, Laura and I go for a walk along new paths - well, new to me and Laura - near to home, which Ed had discovered. There are horses, sheep and cows and views towards the sea a-plenty. I had been snapping away for half an hour before I noticed an error message on my camera - unfortunately I had forgotten to take its SD card out of my laptop and to replace it in the camera. It happens! - not very often, but it happens - and it will be the first walk during the pandemic, if memory serves me correctly, where I have not made a photographic record. This is a source of amusement to Laura and Ed, but I'm just relieved I found out my mistake in the first 30 minutes!

I make a promise to myself to repeat the walk in the next seven days with Beth - she declined today's walk - with a fully-charged battery and the SD card slot double-checked before I leave the house. The animals sell the walk to her and I am confident we will be able to do it before the week is out.

The four of us sit outside in the heat and bright sunshine. We order a takeaway which Laura goes a very short distance to collect when they ring to tell her its ready. We dine al fresco with kebabs, pizzas, a burger. There's beer and wine and all is good with us for a time.

Some of the more obscure TV channels, including some that Laura and I watch regularly, went AWOL this morning - I wonder if it's linked to moving satellites and the launch of the NASA / Space-X rocket which is bound for the International Space Station (ISS). The abbreviation may well end up being superfluous - I don't think I'll mention it again!

It takes me back to the moon landings of 1969 which (I may have imagined) I witnessed with my grand-parents on a small black and white TV - I was 7 and a half, so I can't be sure. Maybe it was a later rocket launch. Whatever it was, I can remember it, or something like it, something - definitely, I'm sure.

I can clearly remember decimalisation in 1971 - now that *really* confused the adults.
I discussed these memories to a bemused family before we went back inside the house.
They knew I was 'old', they know my age, but that gives some sort of context to it.
Beth was especially amused to hear about three-penny bits!
Happy days!

In Scotland, on 12th October 2021, *The Herald* reported:
"Flu and respiratory diseases contributed to a bigger spike in winter deaths three years ago *(2017-18)* than that recorded during December to March this year, in spite of the Covid outbreak. Scotland recorded the second highest seasonal increase in mortality for more than 20 years last winter, according to a new report from the National Records of Scotland (NRS), with Covid blamed for almost two thirds of the additional deaths. However, the increase was actually lower compared to the 2017/18 winter..."

You **REALLY COULD** be forgiven for thinking we had something very similar to Covid-19 in the Winter of 2017-18!

<*I added the info in this box to here in 2022*>

'Time-travelling Scientists Bound For Covid-17 In A Hastily-Constructed Rocket' - 2022

DAY 64

Sunday 31st May 2020

A former nightclub in Workington burned down in the early hours of this morning. The fire had started late last night. I watched a video on Facebook, filmed by the camera phone of a bystander. It showed a huddle of people excitedly watching and what appeared to be a carload of people being dropped off to join in watching. You could hear people bemoaning the loss of a building that held memories, whilst putting the lives of themselves and others at risk by their lack of social distancing.

The fire brigade eventually puts out the fire and, thankfully, no-one died in the blaze, but who knows what the lasting damage of this incident might be?

I wrote these Haiku:

Gawpers

Fire gawpers in Town
Lack of social distancing
Wonder who will die?

Huddle

A huddle of fools
Get their priorities wrong
Mem'ries in ashes

Total deaths from Coronavirus as of yesterday (30/5/20):
USA - 105,557 (331)
UK - 38,376 (68)
Italy - 33,340 (60)
Brazil - 28,834 (212)
France - 28,714 (65)
Spain - 27,125 (47)
Belgium - 9,453 (12)
Mexico - 9,415 (129)
Germany - 8,600 (84)
Iran - 7,734 (84)
Worldwide - 370,506
Number in brackets is population rounded to nearest million.

New Coronavirus deaths announced yesterday :
USA - 1,015 (331)
Brazil - 890 (212)
Mexico - 371 (129)
UK - 215 (68)
India - 205 (1379)
Russia - 181 (146)
Peru - 141 (33)

Italy - 111 (60)
Canada - 94 (38)
Pakistan - 78 (220)
Worldwide - 4,084
Number in brackets is population rounded to nearest million.

Deaths per 1M population (where total deaths are 100+) as of yesterday:
Belgium - 816 (5,022)
Spain - 580 (6,124)
UK - 566 (4,021)
Italy - 551 (3,848)
France - 441 (2,890)
Sweden - 435 (3,677)
Netherlands - 347 (2,700)
Ireland - 335 (5,054)
USA - 319 (5,492)
Switzerland - 222 (3,566)
Worldwide - 47.5 (789)
Number in brackets is cases per 1M population.

Source: Worldometer

Dan Brown, author of *The Da Vinci Code* etc. (or one of his representatives) posts the following:

"Keep your face always toward the sunshine - and shadows will fall behind you."
- Walt Whitman, who was born today in 1819. <end>

It may well be the anniversary of his birth, but that quote seems misplaced today. But maybe it should not be, maybe it is just me who cannot relate to it at this particular moment.

Before I saw this I had already typed the following on Facebook:

Ever feel like you're watching sparks being made in a firework factory?

And this:
Today is Day 64 - the start of Week 10 of my Coronavirus diary which I started about 6 days in to the UK lockdown.
I also have a photographic record of my walks - here is perhaps the most poignant of the photos I've taken. It shows a Christmas wreath still attached to a remembrance bench in Silloth in mid-May (see page 112, top right).

I don't think we're nearing the end of this pandemic (even though lockdown is easing) and I will be continuing to write until it feels the right time to stop.

Rest In Peace all those who have died since the start of the pandemic - whatever the cause.

<end>

I omitted yesterday's blunder with the SD card - I may rectify that.

I also shared an article from *The Guardian* about W.B .Yeats's poem 'The Second Coming'. It is a masterpiece that always resonates at times like this - pretty much the gist of the article - and one that has been my favourite since I studied it at school in my teens. It has been an inspiration to some of my own poems.

It would be ludicrous to suggest the spirit of W.B.Yeats used me as a conduit in my late teens to carry on his work, but he was definitely the driving force behind my 'automatic writing' - that which I used to scribble down when I woke up during the night, then tried to make sense of in the morning.

....

The Second Coming - by W.B.YEATS

Turning and turning in the widening gyre

The falcon cannot hear the falconer;

Things fall apart; the centre cannot hold;

Mere anarchy is loosed upon the world,

The blood-dimmed tide is loosed, and everywhere

The ceremony of innocence is drowned;

The best lack all conviction, while the worst

Are full of passionate intensity.

Surely some revelation is at hand;

Surely the Second Coming is at hand.

The Second Coming! Hardly are those words out

When a vast image out of Spiritus Mundi

Troubles my sight: somewhere in the sands of the desert

A shape with lion body and the head of a man,

A gaze blank and pitiless as the sun,

Is moving its slow thighs, while all about it

Reel shadows of the indignant desert birds.

The darkness drops again; but now I know

That twenty centuries of stony sleep

Were vexed to nightmare by a rocking cradle,

And what rough beast, its hour come round at last,

Slouches towards Bethlehem to be born?

RAPE (excerpt)
Barely noticeable amongst the rush-hour mayhem, but surely no mistake,

A black limousine pulls over and a dark shape shuffles in.

He could have sworn he heard the words the Beast uttered on the wind a-whistling:

"Take me to Bethlehem".

....

A few days ago a black American named George Floyd lost his life at the hands of the police. There has been peaceful protest, but also some violence and looting across the USA for several nights. There have been peaceful protests here in Trafalgar Square and outside the US Embassy in London.

Whilst I can sympathise with the protesters and totally condemn the death of Mr. Floyd, I desperately hope it remains peaceful and groups do not latch on to it with the sole intent of causing damage or looting for personal profit or for 'kicks' - rather than raising awareness, expressing solidarity or effecting change. There is already enough for us to worry about here in the UK.

Although...the potentially negative aspects aside, isn't it amazing how the unjust death of one black American can unite so many and motivate so many into protest when the death of nearly 40,000 people in the UK so far - some would say so many of them so needlessly, due to too little action, too late - has failed to do so?

I almost breathe a sigh of relief that people still *care enough*.

DAY 65

Monday 1st June 2020

The day started reasonably well then went downhill a bit. It's probably all my fault and everyone is still talking to each other - it's really no big deal. So why mention it? It's just to highlight how fragile and unpredictable our moods can be. We can go day to day not being able to predict what mood we are going to wake up in, but we can also wake up in a state of perilous equilibrium. I googled it - 'perilous equilibrium'. It has been used frequently. It's even been used with the start of each word capitalised too! Possibly it's military parlance.

Laura and I had mugs of tea (and I had toast and marmalade) sat outside in the shade - it's always shady in the most private part of our outside space until later in the afternoon and I update my Coronavirus stats. I won't post them here today, but the most positive thing about Sunday's low numbers announcement is that the UK has dropped several places in terms of new deaths. I am pleased NOT to discover any reports of things turning sour at any 'George Floyd' protests in London. There has still been plenty going on in USA, however. Apparently the Trumps may have briefly been in a bunker for part of the weekend - and it's nothing to do with golf! There have been fires burning outside the White House.

After sitting outside for an hour I start to feel a bit chilly in the shade and go back inside the house. A neighbour down the hill is in the bright sunshine with his top off, happily working away in his garden. Maybe Walt Whitman had a point after all.

The latest UK daily Coronavirus death toll is announced as 111 and a 'new low' - lowest since the peak. Tomorrow's figure (shown here on 3/6) will be much more meaningful.

Photo taken in Maryport on 3rd June 2020

DAY 66

Tuesday 2nd June 2020

Today is the 10th anniversary of the (West) Cumbria shootings. A lone gunman shot dead 12 innocent people and wounded 11 others, before turning his weapon on himself. I post the following on my Facebook page alongside a photograph, replacing one of Whitehaven - the largest town he visited on his killing spree - with one showing the 12 victims:

10 years ago today since the fatal shooting of 12 innocent people in West Cumbria and the wounding of 11 others. We will never fully know what motivated Derrick Bird to carry out this atrocity, we can only hope we never see the likes of it again in our peaceful county.

May the 12 victims Rest In Peace.

<end>

I thought it unwise to include Bird himself in the victim numbers. I also thought it unwise to mention the conspiracy theory, associated with the killings, by Richard D. Hall. It suggests a different motivation than Bird having some grudges against some of his initial targets. I will not go into it any further other than to say it starts off very interestingly.

Worldometer's new Coronavirus deaths announced yesterday:
Brazil - 732 (212)
USA - 730 (331)
India - 200 (1379)
Russia - 162 (146)
Mexico - 151 (129)

Peru - 128 (33)
UK - 111 (68)
Iran - 81 (84)
Pakistan - 60 (220)
Italy - 60 (60)
Worldwide - 3,053
Number in brackets is population rounded to nearest million.

I give Ed a lift to Halfords so he can get a new inner tube and tyre for his bicycle - his bike rides are very important to him whilst he is unable to exercise down the gym. There is a queue outside. I catch up with BBC Radio Cumbria to pass the time. I used to listen often when in the car. I'd call myself a regular listener and it's my station of choice, but it's the first time in ages since I've listened to it for more than a few minutes.

A discussion about the weather forecast and the promise of a possible shower or two, gives me an idea and prompts me to write an assortment of very similar Haiku poems.

I post the following one:

Heatwave

Summer time in Spring
Saplings thirsty for water
Dancing when it rains

Here are the other Haiku I wrote on 2nd June 2020:

Children aren't dancing / Summer replaced spring this year / Saplings have wilted

Summertime takes Spring / Saplings are thirsty for rain / Dancing like children

Summer replaced Spring / Excited children dancing / Saplings thirst for rain

I put this in the comment box below the poem:

I didn't think "I wrote this Haiku whilst waiting in Halfords car park listening to BBC Radio Cumbria's weather forecast with a small dead bird in the grill of Laura's car" was such a good introduction, so I'll just leave it here.
<end>

I only noticed the dead bird in the grill when we got home. I removed it with a plastic bag on my hand and disposed of it in the black bin.

The cats looked at me accusingly.

The day ends with a narrow Scrabble victory over Beth.

DAY 67

Wednesday 3rd June 2020

After an uneasy night - Laura and I fell out during foreplay after I refused to follow orders - I wake up wrestling with the black dog. It was no subsitute for a wrestle with Laura *at all*.

I get up late, have poached eggs on toasted buns (with a Best Before date of today) for breakfast, and post the following on Facebook within the space of an hour:

UK now has 2nd most Covid-19 deaths Worldwide *AND* 2nd most deaths per 1M population (where deaths 100+). Source: Worldometer

Total deaths from Coronavirus as of yesterday (2/6/20):
USA - 108,059 (331)
UK - 39,369 (68)
Italy - 33,530 (60)
Brazil - 31,278 (212)
France - 28,940 (65)
Spain - 27,127 (47) - no change
Mexico - 10,167 (129)
Belgium - 9,505 (12)
Germany - 8,674 (84)
Iran - 7,942 (84)
Worldwide - 381,859
Number in brackets is population rounded to nearest million.

New Coronavirus deaths announced yesterday:
Brazil - 1,232 (212)
USA - 1,134 (331)
UK - 324 (68)
Mexico - 237 (129)
India - 221 (1379)
Russia - 182 (146)
Peru - 133 (33)
France - 107 (65)
Pakistan - 78 (220)
Chile - 75
Worldwide - 4,669
Number in brackets is population rounded to nearest million.

Deaths per 1M population (where total deaths are 100+) as of yesterday:
Belgium - 820 (5,059)
UK - 580 (4,097)
Spain - 580 (6,139)
Italy - 555 (3,862)
France - 443 (2,319)
Sweden - 443 (3,823)
Netherlands - 348 (2,723)
Ireland - 336 (5,081)
USA - 327 (5,686)
Switzerland - 222 (3,569)
Worldwide - 49 (826)
Number in brackets is cases per 1M population.   Source: Worldometer

Notes: Elaborate on Best Before date - make a joke. 60% of people not had sex during lockdown due to being apart. *(I made the aforementioned notes, but didn't elaborate on them*.)*

It feels bad to be almost semi-rejoicing in my Facebook post, but it is somewhat of a relief to see us join Spain on 580 deaths per 1M population as I had predicted - it was obvious, it didn't actually take any working out - that we would be over-taking Spain shortly.

Note: Comment and brief discussion with a local celebrity. *(*ditto.)*

Notes: Walk with Laura on prom and south pier.
Angry with Ed over a regency pork pie. About much more than that really.
Go lie on my bed for rest of day, listening to TD, typing up my diary.
Feel inadequate as a step-father, not same as being a real dad, feel I've lost the respect of the kids but never really had it anyway. *(*ditto)*

I would gladly volunteer to die tomorrow if it was to be the last Covid-19 death.

MARYPORT - 3/6/20

MARYPORT - 3/6/20

DAY 68

Thursday 4th June 2020

Total deaths from Coronavirus as of yesterday (3/6/20):
USA - 109,142 (331); UK - 39,728 (68); Italy - 33,601 (60); Brazil - 32,547 (212); France - 29,021 (65); Spain - 27,128 (47); Mexico - 10,637 (129); Belgium - 9,522 (12); Germany - 8,699 (84); Iran - 8,012 (84); Worldwide - 386,787
Number in brackets is population rounded to nearest million.

New Coronavirus deaths announced yesterday:
Brazil - 1,269 (212); USA - 1,083 (331); Mexico - 470 (129); UK - 359 (68); India - 259 (1379); Russia - 178 (146); Peru - 127 (33); Canada - 103 (38); Chile - 87 (19); France - 81 (65); Worldwide - 4,928
Number in brackets is population rounded to nearest million.

Deaths per 1M population (where total deaths are 100+) as of yesterday:
Belgium - 822 (5,065); UK - 585 (4,124); Spain - 580 (6,147); Italy - 556 (3,867); Sweden - 450 (4,042); France - 445 (2,324); Netherlands - 349 (2,728); Ireland - 336 (5,090); USA - 330 (5,748); Switzerland - 222 (3,571); Worldwide - 49.6 (842)
Number in brackets is cases per 1M population.

Source: Worldometer

Ed has an interview for a job with 4 p.m. - 8 p.m. shifts at B&M - ideal to fit around his brief return to school on 14th June and the Summer holidays, I shout "good luck" as he goes out with his mum. Laura is giving him a lift and combining it with a shopping trip. It's the first time I've communicated with him since the 'pork pie incident'.

News about the pandemic and the George Floyd death protests have been, somewhat remarkably, brushed aside for news from Germany regarding a development relating to an ongoing missing child case in Praia Da Luz, Portugal, in 2007. We are made aware of a suspected child killer called Christian B. (Christian Brueckner). The German authorities believe that Madeleine McCann is dead - "No shit Sherlock!" - and that the already imprisoned Christian B, now aged 43, is the killer.

Good news! Ed did well in his interview and gets the job offered to him there and then. He accepts. We make our peace, he gives me £20 that he owes me and I give him it back before the end of the day. He gives me a bottle of *Crabbie's Alcoholic Ginger Beer* (bought via his mum with his own money!) as a peace offering and I reluctantly accept it. At some point - I forget the exact order of events - Ed apologised about the pork pie and I said it wasn't really about that, without me actually saying it was because he deliberately went out of his way to disobey me and did it in an 'arsey' manner. I managed to do it without feeling the need to apologise for me being equally 'arsey' too by going into a big sulk, i.e. keeping out of everyone's way. I think it was a fair exchange and we had a good catch-up to make up for lost time. I even offered to buy him a new mountain-bike, but he declined - preferring to buy a pre-assembled new wheel for his old one as the new tyre and inner-tube he had bought the other day hadn't resolved the problem he's been having with it.

I enjoy the company of Beth later and she shares with me an example of her writing - a short story with an interesting twist. I have been given permission to share it with my poetry group as long as she remains anonymous and I do not modify it in any way. I will have to exercise the same restraint with that as I have done by resisting the urge to share a meme mocking Boris Johnson, announcing that total UK Covid deaths for Wednesday exceeded the total of all 27 countries in the EU combined.

Yes, that's no joke. A total of 359 UK Coronavirus deaths on Wednesday, 3rd June 2020 exceeded the combined total of those announced for that of the remaining 27 EU countries for that day.

Photos taken in Maryport on 8th June 2020

DAY 69

Friday 5th June 2020

Laura and I make up for the other night - nudge, nudge, wink wink! Does no-one use that *Monty Python* line any more? Gosh, I'm showing my age. Stupid old man. She made tea and toast with jam for us in the early hours of the morning. I guess it would have been 4 a.m. when we got to sleep.

I wake up before my 07.45 alarm and put the bins out and feed the cats, taking a cup of tea back to bed with me. We got up together about 11.00 and I made myself hearty bacon sandwiches for brunch.

I typed up and posted my usual Coronavirus stats and gave Ed a lift to work for the start of his induction at B&M.

Total deaths from Coronavirus as of yesterday (4/6/20):
USA - 110,173 (331); UK - 39,904 (68); Brazil - 34,039 (212); Italy - 33,689 (60); France - 29,065 (65); Spain - 27,133 (47); Mexico - 11,729 (129); Belgium - 9,548 (12); Germany - 8,736 (84); Iran - 8,071 (84); Worldwide - 392,298
Number in brackets is population rounded to nearest million.

New Coronavirus deaths announced yesterday:
Brazil - 1,492 (212); Mexico - 1,092 (129); USA - 1,031 (331); India - 275 (1379); UK - 176 (68); Russia - 169 (146); Canada - 139 (38); Peru - 137 (33); Italy - 88 (60); Pakistan - 82 (221); Worldwide - 5,511
Number in brackets is population rounded to nearest million.

Deaths per 1M population (where total deaths are 100+) as of yesterday:
Belgium - 824 (5,072); UK - 588 (4,151); Spain - 580 (6,154); Italy - 557 (3,870); Sweden - 452 (4,149); France - 445 (2,336); Netherlands - 350 (2,740); Ireland - 337 (5,096); USA - 333 (5,815); Switzerland - 222 (3,574); Worldwide - 50.3 (859)
Number in brackets is cases per 1M population.
Source: Worldometer

BBC news alerts me to the fact that the UK death toll has now exceeded 40,000 with 357 new deaths announced today. I note the discrepancies - I sense an imminent adjustment to total deaths may be in the offing. On 6th June it's showing as 40,465.

In other news: It irks me that the Madeleine McCann case has made the news headlines for the third day running.

There is only one lectern at the daily Coronavirus briefing. Only Health Secretary, Matt Hancock, makes an appearance. He gives his announcement and takes the Q&As completely alone. That is not something Boris has managed to do single-handedly throughout the entire Pandemic.

Most of my evening is spent finishing off a poem I have been writing about the last mud-horse fisherman, Adrian Sellick, who, along with his father Brendan (and many generations before them) carried out the craft in Bridgwater Bay in Somerset, under the glare of the Hinkley Point Powerstation.

'The Last Mud-Horse Fisherman'
Ink Drawing 2022

DAY 70

Saturday 6th June 2020

I while away the time doing some research for current and future poems: reading news articles, watching old interviews and footage on Youtube. I have a brief online chat with my mate Steven - we hope to meet up and do a photography walk soon at Allonby, maybe.

I spent a couple of hours with Laura (and the kids for part of the time) sat out enjoying the warmth of the late afternoon sunshine - me having a few small bottles of beer. Laura rang in an order to our favourite chinese fast food establishment in town and went out forty minutes later to collect it. Every precaution had been taken to minimise risk to public health in the process, but I did go halves when it came to payment.

The UK daily death toll is announced as 204. Worldwide deaths have now exceeded 400,000.

Total deaths from Covid19 to date:
1st USA - 111,658 (pop. 351M)
2nd UK - 40,465 (pop. 68M)
3rd Brazil - 35,211 (pop. 212M)
4th Italy - 33,846 (pop. 60M)
Worldwide - 400,024
Source: Worldometer - 18.50 6/6/20

Laura informs me that the R rate in the North-West of England is 1.01.

There has been no daily Coronavirus briefing today - Boris has stopped them taking place at weekends.

'Boris the Weekend Werewolf' Cosplay kit - £2.99

Also available: 'COUNT BORIS - ZE VEEKEND VAMPIRE' - £4.99

DAY 71

Sunday 7th June 2020

We get up late - apart from Ed who was up at 09.30 for a run. Laura and I have cups of tea and three (!) toasted hot cross buns each with lashings of butter. Mmmmm!

Laura has been reading lots of books in the last couple of weeks - ones bought and put away for 'holiday reading'. She enjoys gory horror thrillers and asks me to find some more for her from her favourite author of the genre, J.A. Konrath. I spend a couple of hours looking round different online sites trying to find bargains. It's hard enough trying to find the books she needs - let alone well-priced ones - and I end up having to spend over £45 on new copies of four of his paperbacks. I am happy to treat her to them though. I will also need to spend £30 on Beth to match what I have spent on Ed lately - the kids are quick to find out what I have spent on the other and are equally quick to make it clear if any unfairness is deemed to have taken place!

On Friday I had treated myself to some digital music purchases from Bandcamp in support of Thorsten Quaeschning from Tangerine Dream. I prefer to buy CDs, but this option is not yet available for his recent performances - I have been enjoying listening to some of his 'live' improvised sessions: 'Behind Closed Doors' with a range of guest artists. I bought tickets for myself and my two daughters to see Tangerine Dream in Manchester in October, but I do not know if this will still go ahead.

There is much for which life is 'on hold' at the moment. Laura and I are both still furloughed. The kids have not returned to school. They have not seen their dad or their grandparents in person since the start of the pandemic - nor I my daughters. Laura has not seen her eldest son and daughter or her mum either.

Three of us are booked on a flight to Majorca in July and that is not looking optimistic. We will not know until a week before whether or not the flight will be cancelled and, if it does, whether or not we will need to quarantine for 14 days on return (which may make it impossible for Laura to travel, due to having to be off work for so long). If we can go on holiday then I will hastily need to find affordable accommodation options.

Then there is the mental and emotional 'paralysis': the procrastinating; the unwillingness to get on with the more important things one could be doing; the bottling up of emotions; the uncertainty of what a return to work will hold; the occasional agoraphobic feeling; the darker thoughts; the self-doubt.

What is the point? What does the future hold? Will things ever be the same again? Why does any of this matter any more? What am I going to do? How will we cope? How will this all end? These may be some of the internal debates swirling round and round in some of our heads. Ones that may be very difficult to share or to articulate. Sadly, some people will already have decided that there is no future for them and will have ended their lives prematurely. Others will have had their lives taken from them prematurely. *Some, like me, will have had far too much thinking time. Regrets? I've had a few!*

I spend quite a bit of the rest of the day re-acquainting myself with some of the evidence in the Portuguese police's files regarding the disappearance of Madeleine McCann, some videos of statement analysis conducted by Peter Hyatt and, for the first time, seek out other 'McCann-related' content on Wikileaks.

It is on Wikileaks that I find a download of Tony Bennett's (Madeleine Foundation) book/pamphlet. It pretty much reaches the same conclusions as that of the former Portuguese police chief, Goncalo Amaral's book: *The Truth Of The Lie*.

The media is full of news again - I forget how many consecutive days that is now - about 'prime suspect' Christian B's possible involvement in Madeleine McCann's disappearance (and that of other missing children). Knowing as much as I do - having previously spent many years studying the case - I remain highly sceptical. I do not believe the truth will ever be allowed to come out, but we may, however, eventually be presented with something else entirely, that is designed to bring some sort of closure.

Meanwhile, the 'Black Lives Matter' protests continue to rage across the World. I am pleased that the ones in the UK have remained largely peaceful.

Photos on Pages 143-146 were taken in Maryport on Monday, 8th June 2020

DAY 72

Monday 8th June 2020

Total deaths from Coronavirus as of yesterday (7/6/20):
USA - 112,469 (331); UK - 40,542 (68); Brazil - 36,499 (212); Italy - 33,899 (60); France - 29,155 (65); Spain - 27,136 (47); Mexico - 13,511 (129); Belgium - 9,595 (12); Germany - 8,776 (84); Iran - 8,281 (84); Worldwide - 405,081
Number in brackets is population rounded to nearest million.

New Coronavirus deaths announced yesterday:
Chile - 649; Brazil - 542 (212); USA - 373 (331); Mexico - 341 (129); India - 261 (1379); Peru - 164 (33); Russia - 134 (146); UK - 77 (68); Iran - 72 (84); Pakistan - 67 (221); Worldwide - 3,382
Number in brackets is population rounded to nearest million.

Deaths per 1M population (where total deaths are 100+) as of yesterday:
Belgium - 828 (5,112); UK - 597 (4,217); Spain - 580 (6,173); Italy - 561 (3,886); Sweden - 462 (4,431); France - 447 (2,359); Netherlands - 351 (2,777); USA - 340 (6,067); Ireland - 340 (5,107); Switzerland - 222 (3,580); Worldwide - 52 (909)
Number in brackets is cases per 1M population.

Source: Worldometer

The morning and early afternoon was an uneventful blur.

I drop Ed off for his first full four-hour shift at work at about 15.50 - this was after Laura's car failed to start, for no apparent reason other than a flat battery. Laura and I park near the harbour and go for a walk. It's a lovely day out and there are more people out than has been usual of late.

I take over 220 photographs and spend the evening editing and working my magic on them on my laptop. Laura and I got someone out to help start her car, but we won't know for sure if it's fixed until we try to start it tomorrow.

Those things are a good distraction from my mental state.

In memory of 3 lives lost at sea
after the capsizing of fishing vessel
Aquila
Bo Faskadale Reef, Ardnamurchan, Scotland
Monday 20th July 2009
Tony Hayton (Skipper) 45
Martin Sanderson 52
Peter (Bubbles) Hilton 52
Three sons of Maryport who never came home.

When winds and tides are rolling in
In silent thoughts you will hear them sing

DAY 73

Tuesday 9th June 2020

Our drains are blocked - it's the second time this year we've had problems with them.

Laura gets a new matching kettle and toaster delivered. Ed gets a new wheel delivered to go on his old bicycle.

Ed walks to work because Laura's car wouldn't start again.

Laura buys a new battery from the very nice AA man. Her car is working fine again.

Laura picks Ed up from work at the end of his shift. She stops on the way home to buy lots of chocolate. She eats a huge bar of Cadbury's *Fruit & Nut* all by herself later, but I only eat a third of my *Whole Nut* bar.

I learn from a friend that Facebook have shut down some Punk and Skinhead sites because someone decided they're all racist. It's been a slow news day!

DAY 74

Wednesday 10th June 2020

Total deaths from Coronavirus as of yesterday (9/6/20):
USA - 114,148 (331); UK - 40,883 (68); Brazil - 38,497 (212); Italy - 34,043 (60); France - 29,296 (65); Spain - 27,136 (47); Mexico - 14.053 (129); Belgium - 9,619 (12); Germany - 8,831 (84); Iran - 8,425 (84); Worldwide - 412,972
Number in brackets is population rounded to nearest million.

New Coronavirus deaths announced yesterday:
Brazil - 1,185 (212); USA - 1,093 (331); Mexico - 354 (129); UK - 286 (68); India - 246 (1379); Russia - 171 (146);   Peru - 167 (33); Pakistan - 105 (221); France - 87 (65); South Africa - 82 (59); Worldwide - 4,732
Number in brackets is population rounded to nearest million.

Deaths per 1M population (where total deaths are 100+) as of yesterday:
Belgium - 830 (5,130); UK - 602 (4,260); Spain - 580 (6,182); Italy - 563 (3,896); Sweden - 467 (4,549); France - 449 (2,369); Netherlands - 352 (2,796); USA - 345 (6,182); Ireland - 343 (5,110); Switzerland - 224 (3,582); Worldwide - 53 (938)
Number in brackets is cases per 1M population.   Source: Worldometer

Ed tried in vain

To fix his bike in the rain

But despite new wheel and all

Same problem, not solved at all

I managed to eventually unblock our drains - using the same drainage rods that failed to unblock them last time I used them, but I managed to attack from both ends this time and got them flowing freely again.

Laura gives Ed a lift to work and goes off to do a 'big shop' at Asda with Beth. I have a bizarre sense of freedom, but I simply have what we call a 'shath' - a shower whilst sat or lying in the bath - make myself a mug of coffee and type this up in silence.

There is an online 'Speakeasy Meets Poets Out Loud' to look forward to at 19.30.

I successfully bid on a second hand Nintendo 3DS bundle for Beth. She's been saying she'd like to get a replacement for two she had stolen from our hotel apartment in Tenerife a few years ago. She should be paying half, but I let her off with it and also treated her to a multi games cartridge with a whopping 468 games for it.

I enjoy the online poetry session via Zoom. I had already decided Beth's piece of prose from the perspective of a terrorist bomber (!) might be too controversial to use. I am reasonably happy with my poem: 'The Last Mud-Horse Fisherman', but my two Haiku form poem contributions seem misplaced, out-of-step somewhat in the light of ongoing Black Lives Matter protests in the wake of the death of George Floyd. The one about people in a huddle gawping at a fire in Workington (seen earlier here) seems pretty petty now in the light of much bigger gatherings across the world. The other, about Mr. Floyd's death bringing us all together in protest where 40,000 deaths due to Coronavirus - 'Clap For Carers' aside? - seemingly didn't, seems wildly optimistic and quite plainly wrong, although it did accurately reflect my mood at the time it was written. That is all poetry can do sometimes - give a snapshot of how one feels in the moment, frozen in time. It can paint a beautiful picture of feeling at one with nature, record an important event in history, give a sense of optimism or be a portent of impending doom.

....

'George Floyd' - Three Verses In Haiku Form

At last a protest
A lone black American
Death troubles many

Where forty-thousand
Only kept us divided
One man's death unites

A peaceful London
Shouts out loud from the rooftops
Won't take any more!

> *What does the ONS tell us now in 2022 about Excess Winter Mortality in Winter 2020-21?*
>
> *An estimated 63,000 EWDs occurred in England and Wales - **6.1 times higher than Winter 2019-20.**
> The EWM Index in England was significantly higher than all winters since the series began in 1991-92.*
>
> **In Wales, HOWEVER, the EWM Index was significantly higher than all years** *since the series began in 1991-92* **EXCEPT 2017-18.**
> *Covid-19 was the leading cause of EWMs in 2020-21 accounting to 84% in England and 82.9% in Wales.*

THE LAST MUD-HORSE FISHERMAN

Well beyond the stone-riddled foreshore,
Distanced from the glare of the huge grey power-monster,
Weighted down by rocks, one mile out decreed,
An ancient, forlorn, but trusty, steed -
A simple wooden construction, built by hand
To safely navigate mud-banks - not sink in, like quicksand.
Now laden with two baskets, a sieve and a walking pole
It is ready to make a mere *half*-journey whole.
Passed down two centuries, a long lost ancient art -
A fifth generation fisherman will surely be the last
Seen sledging through the mud, belly to the plank,
Riding far beyond the distant edge of the bladder-wrack.

Two miles out now, at tide's lowest ebb, he's staking out the nets -
Traditionally, of hemp and twine; meagre pickings, he now expects.
Brown shrimp his main catch, from April 'til first frost -
A salty sea tang potted feast - to sell in the cottage shop.
Perhaps a sea bass or a Dover sole, whitebait - and cod in the winter.
The purses or cod ends, as sometimes called, spill out no riches' glitter.
Among the shrimp though, there's an increasingly rare eel,
Then a couple of skates and a haul of sprats is revealed.

He fears no-one is willing to climb aboard and take the reins,
There's much better livelihoods, they think, than this one to be made.
Gliding over deep mud in a treacherous location -
Too hard and dirty the work, too little the remuneration.

Acres of brown, slippery sea-weed fringe a vast expanse -
A grey, sea-washed nothingness in which to eke a living, what chance
Against the menacing bulk's lure of jobs and gargantuan water intake?
Hold fast tradition, anchor the heart, for history's sake!

I dedicate this page to Brendan Sellick who passed away peacefully on 10th August 2021, aged 86.

DAY 75

Thursday 11th June 2020

I could have got up at 07.30, but I decide to try to get back to sleep at 08.00 and eventually get up at 11.30, feeling very tired. I cannot explain the science behind why I felt less tired at 07.30.

Laura and I sat outside reading books for an hour or so. I stop to watch a murder of crows circling above us - some stopping temporarily on the highest branches of a tall tree slightly higher up the hill, before rejoining their accomplices. I alert Laura to the sight as their numbers swell, the circle enlarges and others drop off to take their turn resting. It is not something I have ever witnessed before. It is starting to look like a scene from Hitchcock's *The Birds*, a crime in the making. We should be fearful of becoming the victims, but I think Laura would be more concerned about the washing that's drying on the line. The crows' restlessness suggests a change in the weather as the sky darkens and the temperature dips and it's not long before we are back inside.

I am currently listening to Nicola Sturgeon's daily Coronavirus briefing. I must admit I am increasingly blurry now on the differences between the four nations of the United Kingdom of Great Britain and Northern Ireland. Everything started to become more blurry after Dominic Cummings's lockdown transgressions and I care much less now about these differences. Laura and I continue to do pretty much what we've been doing since the start. We respect the rules and take sensible precautions to minimise risk to both ourselves and others - as do the children, save for Ed recently starting his first job and, therefore, introducing a new element of risk.

Ed informs me he has agreed to do 10 hours over-time next week - the job must be going well. I'm not sure he'll cope as well when he returns to school on Monday (or is it Monday 22nd as Laura thinks?) and when the gym reopens later in the Summer.

Photos on Pages 150-151 were taken in Maryport on Monday, 8th June 2020

DAY 76

Friday 12th June 2020

Ok, I'll skip the reason for getting up at 07.45. I go back to bed at 08.15, cats fed and last night's dishes watched. Laura's midnight promise to have us up early has not materialised. She ignores me when I ask if she wants me to bring her up a cup of tea. Her 9 a.m. alarm comes and goes. She gets up late and I get up even later. The only thing I can say in our defence is that we probably didn't get to sleep until after 2 a.m. The other night it would have been about 4 a.m. We do spend a lot more time out of bed than it, but we are lazier at this stage of the lockdown than we were before it or in the early part of it.

I think the main reason we spend more time in bed than we used to is a mental thing - it's a defence mechanism, a way to protect ourselves from having to think too much, to worry too much, having to consume more crazy news than our brains can handle and to have less of our days to fill. Sleep and dreams seem better bed-follows than they've ever been before - especially since the nightmares have stopped.

It's been a miserable-looking day, but I'm pleased to report that Beth has been out and *is* getting out a lot more and is meeting up with a friend to enjoy shared walks since the lockdown eased. We have not, however, had the 'new' walk together that we agreed to do and it remains the only one not photographed by me.

I make sure Ed's dinner is ready when he gets in from work at 8 p.m. - meatballs with spaghetti in a tangy tomato sauce. He announces that he's doing six hours tomorrow instead of having two days off. It's great to see someone keen to get back to work! I think it will be a good few weeks before I'm back interviewing people in their homes. Laura is due to start back at work around the same time in July as we are due to fly to Majorca for a two-week holiday.

DAY 77

Saturday 13th June 2020

I embroil myself - as I have done many times in the past - into 'recent developments' in the Madeleine McCann case. I won't bore anyone else with the details.

Later, three of us will get a takeaway delivered. Unfortunately they will miss out the chilli sauce from my doner kebab order - chilli flakes out of the cupboard will be a poor substitute.

It is late afternoon when my beautiful Laura - freshly showered, hair done (as much as it can be done when in lockdown) and a little make-up applied - seduces me and lures me away from my laptop and out into the sunshine.

EPILOGUE

That was my final diary entry - despite lockdown continuing in various forms for some considerable time thereafter. If I could have added to it, I'd have added something along the lines of the following:

'I miss the spice in my life - we all do. We've all had the spice taken out of our lives in one way or another recently. What's left behind is bland and repetitive and safe. There is some comfort in that, but we must now learn how to break away from that comfort. We must learn how to live again.'

I start typing this closing section in the second quarter of 2022. There has been much during the time of writing my diary - and subsequently - that has shocked and angered the British public. Dominic Cummings, Matt Hancock, Rishi Sunak and Boris Johnson have all struggled, at various times, to follow the Coronavirus guidelines laid down by this Conservative government. In April 2022 Boris became the first ever serving UK Prime Minister to be fined for breaking the law and yet he remained in office. Similarly, Rishi Sunak became the first serving Chancellor to suffer the same fate. Tory MP Neil Parish later resigned for twice watching pornography on his phone in the House of Commons. The High Court ruled - also in April 2022 - that the Government acted unlawfully when it sent hospital patients into care homes without testing them for Covid.

Meanwhile, well over 150,000 people in the UK to date have either died from Coronavirus or within 28 days of a positive Covid test. Over 150,000 families have lost loved ones - many without being given the opportunity to say goodbye.

I am very grateful that all of my family survived the pandemic. We are coping - both mentally and financially. We still live in the same house in Maryport - me, Laura and her two youngest, my step-children, Ed and Beth. We did, however, have to spend several months in a rental property after our house got flooded in August 2020.

I was delighted to finally get to see the new line-up of Tangerine Dream, live in concert at the RNCM Manchester, at the third time of asking in March 2022 - spending a lovely time with my daughters, Charlotte and Becky.

Beth has had her 18th birthday, is about to complete her 6th form studies and has started working part-time. Ed has embarked on a degree apprenticeship and now owns his first car - having sailed through his test first time. Laura has changed to a job with reduced hours that gives her more quality time with us all.

Shortly after the death of his father Brendan, Adrian Sellick announced his retirement from Mud-Horse Fishing.

I wondered what might have happened to the fictional ex-soldier and his wife during lockdown and wrote some final words, based on my poem 'On The Eve', under a different title to those that I'd written earlier:

ON THE EVE OF HIS FUNERAL

It's quite ironic really - he used to go on and on

About that big flaming red Brexit bus with all of them numbers on.

What them lying buggers said we'd save to spend on't NHS.

Then along comes Covid, you can't get an appointment, your ops are cancelled - it's such a bloody mess.

Oh, sorry mum, I'm gonna have to go - that'll be vicar come early I bet.

Hello vicar, come on in, you'll have to excuse the state it's in - I've not had a chance to tidy yet.

I decided to drop kids off at his mum's before I went to see 'Undertaker Jim'.

But it'll be all sorted for coming back to tomorrow after we've said our goodbye to him.

My mum's coming round later to help. He'll get a better send-off than he really deserves.

She's gonna splash the cash in M&S - we're even having h'ors d'oeuvres.

It'll be back to food bank next week. Me? I'm doing ok.

Doc's loaded me up with tablets for my nerves.

I'm sorry if I look a sight.

I'm coping alright...considering.

And I'm hoping, after tomorrow night,

That I'll come out of it a bit better.

Better than I am today

And better than how I've been.

Oh he'd really been hell to live with for some of the lockdown time

And when I got depression and struggled to cope, he turned to petty crime.

I turned a blind eye and it got us by until he started back on't drink.

He went berserk when news of the parties broke, and although he'd never used his fists, I'd dodged everything bar the kitchen sink

And one time a saucepan connected and I ended up in A&E

And I'd had to tell lies to protect him because I knew that he still loved me.

And as long as he did still love me, I'd try my very best to love him.

And I still do - despite what he's done.

It's funny, it's recorded as a Covid death because he'd had a positive one.

A test - I mean - two weeks before. Two weeks before he jumped,

Pissed as a fart, in front of that bus, the stupid bloody lump.

A big red double-decker bus. You couldn't make it up!

You could not make it up!

That poor lady driving it. I took her some flowers - hoping to bring her some cheer.

Fat chance - he's ruined her life n'all. She was totally bereft.

I told her "Oh no, it wasn't your fault my dear."

And showed her the note that he'd left.

I think that only made things worse.

And it has made things worse, I think.

She won't be there tomorrow.

Bless her!

....

I am considering retiring following a busy 18 months or so working full-time on behalf of the ONS Covid Infection Study as a Swab Worker. This involved asking volunteer participants survey questions and collecting swab and (later) blood samples, on their doorsteps, for sending on to labs to test for the virus and antibodies respectively. The job threw me a financial lifeline and I loved the work. I never thought I would ever feel well enough to return to full-time employment.

Laura and I consider ourselves very fortunate to have enjoyed foreign holidays in July 2020 (with Beth) and October 2021.

Finally, I would like to thank everyone who has bought and/or read through this book. Thank you for your patience and for putting up with me. It feels like an honest and accurate, imperfect by necessity, 'warts-and-all' account - a madman's social commentary if you will - and I sincerely hope you did find some enjoyment or benefit from following this journey.

It had not been my original intention to publish this work anonymously and to disguise (to some extent) my and my family's identities, but I had to bow to pressure and it was either this or perhaps not be able to publish at all.

Please rest assured that I don't mean anyone any harm from this work. I only wish you peace, love and happiness. Oh, and good health - lots of it!

I found this chair, exactly as pictured, on the shore between Flimby and Maryport, on 24th August 2020

A Moment, Swimming

Playa Del Cura, Gran Canaria, October 2021

As we approached
the beach
  from the sea
    and you tried to find
    a safe place
    for your feet,
      all you could see,
      before the
      inevitable
      grounding
        in volcanic sand,
        was a long seam
        of dark rock
        on the murky,
        churning sea-bed.
      That was
      until I told you
      that the blackness
      was just the shadow
      that your body cast
    and we laughed
    as your feet hit sand
    and I took your hand
    as we tried to dodge
  the breakers,
 together,
in the sunshine.

INDEX OF POEMS AND QUOTES

Page:	
1	BILLY
2	EVEREST
3	VARIATION ON A THEME BY RILKE by DENISE LEVERTOV - *The Book Of Hours, Book 1, Poem 1, Stanza 1*
7	RISE AND SET
8	UP-HILL by CHRISTINA ROSSETTI
13	From DEVOTIONS UPON EMERGENT OCCASIONS (excerpt) by JOHN DONNE
14	LIGHT OF HOPE
15	HURDLER
15	SOCKGATE by LAURA
16	GREY, BLACK, SHADOW
16	STAY HOME! by LAURA
22	CRAIG by LAURA
27	AUGURIES OF INNOCENCE (excerpt) by WILLIAM BLAKE
35	MY HEART LEAPS UP WHEN I BEHOLD by WILLIAM WORDSWORTH
36	SLOW, FRIENDS, AUSSIES, SWALEDALE, COLLECTORS (5 Hay(na)ku)
61	BRAVE OLD SEQUENCE (excerpt)
65	TOWARDS MOCKERKIN (excerpt)
74	JACK AND MARGUERITE (excerpt)
88-90	ON THE EVE
94	THE LAKES REMEMBER (excerpt)
103	SUMMER RAIN
107-108	LARKS' TONGUES IN ASPIC
119	SONGS, A MARS BAR ADVERT AND CASABLANCA CORRECTLY QUOTED
120	TIME TO KILL?
127	GAWPERS, HUDDLE (2 Haiku)
129	THE SECOND COMING by W.B.YEATS
129	RAPE (excerpt)
132	HEATWAVE, CHILDREN, SUMMERTIME, SUMMER (4 Haiku)
148	GEORGE FLOYD - Three Verses In Haiku Form
149	THE LAST MUD-HORSE FISHERMAN
154-155	ON THE EVE OF HIS FUNERAL
157	A MOMENT, SWIMMING